# THE GREAT COMPOSERS
## THEIR LIVES AND TIMES

# A Guide to

# *Classical Music*

# Staff Credits

### Editors
David Buxton BA (Honours)
Sue Lyon BA (Honours)

### Art Editors
Debbie Jecock BA (Honours)
Ray Leaning BA (Honours),
PGCE (Art & Design)

### Deputy Editor
Barbara Segall BA

### Sub-editors
Geraldine Jones
Judy Oliver BA (Honours)
Nigel Rodgers BA (Honours), MA
Penny Smith
Will Steeds BA (Honours), MA

### Designers
Steve Chilcott BA (Honours)
Shirin Patel BA (Honours)
Chris Rathbone

### Picture Researchers
Georgina Barker
Julia Calloway BA (Honours)
Vanessa Cawley

### Production Controllers
Sue Fuller
Steve Roberts

### Secretary
Lynn Smail

### Publisher
Terry Waters Grad IOP

### Editorial Director
Maggi McCormick

### Production Executive
Robert Paulley BSc

### Managing Editor
Alan Ross BA (Honours)

### Consultants
Dr Antony Hopkins
Commander of the Order
of the British Empire,
Fellow of the
Royal College of Music

Nick Mapstone BA (Honours), MA

Keith Shadwick BA (Honours)

**Reference Edition Published 1990**

Published by Marshall Cavendish Corporation
147 West Merrick Road
Freeport, Long Island
N.Y. 11520

Typeset by Walkergate Press Ltd, Hull, England
Printed and bound in Singapore by
Times Offset Private Ltd.

© Marshall Cavendish Limited MCMLXXXIV,
MCMLXXXVII, MCMXC.

**Library of Congress Cataloging-in-Publication Data**

The Great composers, their lives and times.

Includes index.
1. Composers—Biography. 2. Music appreciation.
I. Marshall Cavendish Corporation.
ML390.G82    1987       780'.92'2 [B]       86-31294
ISBN 0-86307-776-5

ISBN 0-86307-776-5 (set)
0-86307-785-4 (vol)

THE
GREAT COMPOSERS
*THEIR LIVES AND TIMES*

# A Guide to
# *Classical Music*

MARSHALL CAVENDISH
LONDON ● NEW YORK ● SYDNEY

THE
# GREAT COMPOSERS
*THEIR LIVES AND TIMES*

# Contents

# Introduction

Like all great art, classical music can be enjoyed in many ways. At its most basic, the repertoire of classical music contains as many memorable, catchy tunes as the great Broadway musicals. Indeed, modern composers have on occasion paid their classical predecessors the compliment of borrowing from their works – for example, the Arabian-Nights fantasy musical, Kismet (filmed by Vincente Minnelli in 1955) is based on themes from the Polovstian Dances by the 19th-century Russian composer, Alexander Borodin. Most kinds of music appeal directly to the emotions, but great music has the greatest power: the majesty of a Beethoven concerto exalts us; the limpidity of a Mozart serenade delights us; and the Romantic sadness of a Tchaikovsky symphony moves us to pity.

However, just as a football game has more meaning – and is more entertaining – if the spectators understand its rules, so classical music will be most truly enjoyed and appreciated only if we know something of its conventions and history. For this reason, this volume contains not only a full glossary of musical terms, but also an account of the historical background to classical music's development and, since no music would exist without the means to play it, an examination of early instruments and the strings, brass, woodwind and percussion instruments that form the modern symphony orchestra.

# A history of classical music

*Bach, Mozart, Beethoven, Tchaikovsky and Stravinsky are all acknowledged to be great composers, but their music not only sounds very different, but is also obviously a product of the 18th, 19th or 20th centuries. This is inevitable, since music, like any other art-form, reflects the spirit of the age in which it is created; so to understand the meaning of a piece of music, we must know something of its historical background, as described in the pages that follow. In Western Europe, much great music was, of course, composed before 1650, when this survey of the eras of classical music begins – the 15th- and 16th-century Renaissance in the visual arts was reflected in music – but the styles of classical music that we know today developed in the dynamic, expanding Europe of the 17th century, and it was also at this time that the modern symphony orchestra began to take shape.*

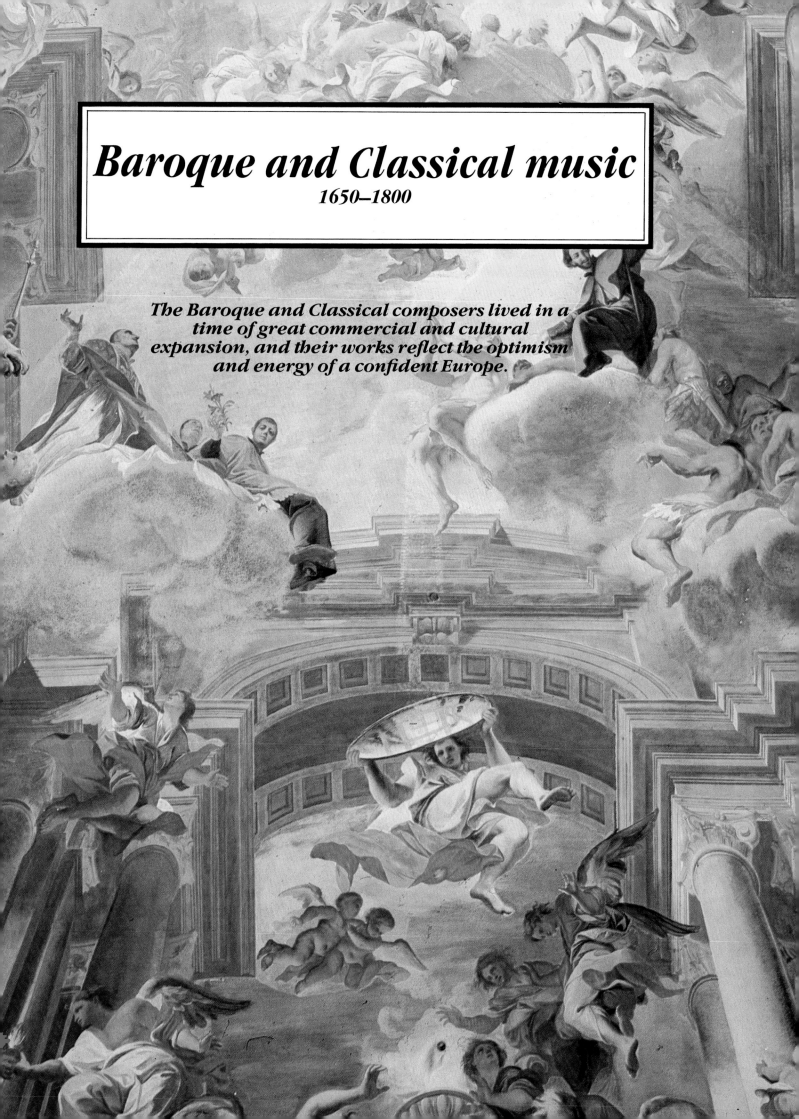

# Baroque and Classical music
### *1650–1800*

*The Baroque and Classical composers lived in a time of great commercial and cultural expansion, and their works reflect the optimism and energy of a confident Europe.*

*Left (text beside image in italic caption):*
*Queen Christina of Sweden enjoys a discussion on geometry with René Descartes, the founder of modern philosophy (above). Christina was eager for knowledge and an outstanding patron of the arts and scholarship.*

*The word 'Baroque' probably originated from a jewellers' term for irregular pearls. They were sometimes made into precious pendants such as the one shown above.*

The word 'Baroque' probably comes from the Portuguese *'barocco'* meaning a misshapen pearl, and can still be used to describe something 'irregular'. The term was first used to describe a sensationally ornamental style in art and architecture, which began in Italy around 1600 and gradually moved north, where it underwent new interpretations and influences in very different – notably German – contexts. So the term 'Baroque' is now generally applied to European culture from the early 17th century to the mid-18th century.

### The Baroque spirit

The Baroque age was a relatively affluent and dynamic period in history. Divided into two more or less permanent camps (Catholicism and Protestantism), Europe was beginning to recover from the religiously-motivated struggles and wars that had followed the Reformation. And although most people were still devoutly Christian, there was a growing feeling that it was not worth persecuting groups or nations with deviant opinions. With the rise of comfortably-off merchant classes, there were more educated people and more private individuals with money to lavish on houses, clothes, art and music. As a result artists, craftsmen and musicians enjoyed a boom time.

Among intellectuals, mathematics became almost an alternative religion, with the proviso, of course, that God was the supreme mathematical genius who had created the world. The French philospher René Descartes (1596–1650) stated his account of the way in which the world worked from a bare principle – 'I think therefore I am' – and he urged seekers of the Truth to cast aside all their preconceptions, including religious convictions, and start from scratch. But there was nothing irreverent about this sort of attitude: it was simply that a phenomenon such as a rainbow could now be enjoyed both as a divine signal and as the product of the refraction of light. Characteristically, the English genius Isaac Newton (1642–1727), who is most famous for having discovered the law of universal gravitation, devoted a great deal of his energy to 'de-coding' the Bible. Although the Creation was undoubtedly complex, there was an optimistic belief that with the aid of mathematics – the only way of uniting reason with lived experience – the inherent harmony or order behind all mysteries could be discovered.

### Rhythm in stone

These two ingredients – complexity and harmony – are central to the Baroque spirit, particularly its architecture and music. The spectacular buildings of the Baroque are characterized by the almost 'rhythmical' relationship between all the spaces within the total complex. Among their most striking features are sweeping staircases, described by one historian as 'veritable triumphs of rhythm in stone', while the elaborate balustrades and façades are 'music become stone'.

So it was in this spirit that the orchestra as an organized body of music-makers took shape. The

*Side credits (rotated):*
Versailles/Telarci-Giraudon
Victoria & Albert Museum, Crown Copyright
Franz Jacob Rousseau 'Masked Ball in the Theatre at Bonn' Kölnisches Stadt Museum

Foundation Willem van der Vorm, Museum Boymans-van Beuningen, Rotterdam

*The Amsterdam stock exchange in 1653 (above). The Baroque age was a time of great commercial expansion and at this time the Dutch bourse was the busiest money market in Europe.*

*A masked ball in the theatre at Bonn (above). Occasions of any kind – operas, concerts, ballets, even funerals, were often a pretext for festive display in the 17th and 18th centuries.*

Baroque composers – among them Vivaldi, Bach and Handel – took account of the strengths and individual characteristics of different instruments in a new way. They were particularly fond of the violin, an instrument that was perfected in Italy by the Amati, Stradivari and Guarneri families between 1650 and 1740. The concerto became a favourite form and in due course this 'concerted effort' evolved into a sonata for several players. Later it developed into a means of displaying the skills of a soloist which achieved a greater contrast between the whole and its parts. Musicians, too, were concerned to present a rich but harmonious complexity.

### Cities and crowds

Baroque composers were catering for a public which was prepared to pay for the music it enjoyed, and many of their patrons were themselves discriminating and capable musicians. This was especially true of aristocratic patrons in the Baroque period, when cultivated 'benevolent despots' were emerging. The Habsburg Charles VI played on the harpsichord at musical recitals and his daughter, Maria Theresa, sang in private operatic performances. In Britain and Hanover the three Georges were ardent admirers of Handel's music, and in Prussia Frederick the Great's enthusiasm for music was such that he often exhausted his royal orchestra with his own interminable flute concertos.

At a popular level also – for the crowds of the towns and cities – music was an important pleasure. Baroque culture was very urban, for it was in this period that many of Europe's leading cities were either built or revamped. The elements we associate with 'showbiz' today – glitter, expense, visual titillation – were very much a part of public entertainments, and composers like Handel catered for the musical taste of their spectators with works such as the *Music for the Royal Fireworks*. Keen rivalry between the 'fans' of different composers stimulated great interest in developments in music and most big towns and cities boasted opera houses and pleasure gardens.

There were two main elements in the Baroque spirit: one exaltingly religious and the other extravagantly pleasurable. And when the pleasurable aspect began to dominate there was a transition to a new intellectual climate – that of the Enlightenment and Classicism. But there was nothing frivolous about this change of emphasis: after all, in the last quarter of the 18th century the 'pursuit of happiness' was thought a proper aim by the founders of the United States of America. Like many other cultivated individuals of their day, the American Founding Fathers were following up on the 'reasonable' tradition, which thinkers like Descartes had started and which flowered as the period in history called the Enlightenment.

# Introduction to the period

*Corelli*

*Albinoni*

*Telemann*

*Bach*

*Haydn*

| DATES: | MUSIC | HISTORY |
|---|---|---|
| **1650-1665** | **Beginnings** of modern harmony (c. 1650)<br>**Overture** introduced to opera (1650)<br>**Minuet** popularized by Lully at French court (1652)<br>**Pachelbel** b. (1653)<br>**Corelli** b. (1653)<br>**Purcell** b. (1659)<br>**Lully** composes for Molière's ballets (1664) | **Portuguese** drive Dutch from Brazil (1654<br>**Oliver Cromwell** d. (1658)<br>**First bank notes** issued in Sweden (1658)<br>**Restoration of Charles II** (1660)<br>**Louis XIV** begins reign (1661)<br>**Bombay** (1661) and New York (1664) acquired by England |
| **1666-1680** | **Stradivarius** labels his violins (1666)<br>**Couperin** writes harpsichord works in form of Programme Music (1668)<br>**Albinoni** b. (1671)<br>**Académie de la Musique** founded (1671)<br>**Vivaldi** b. (1678)<br>**Purcell** becomes organist at Westminster Abbey (1679) | **Great Fire** of London (1666)<br>**Gobelins** workshops established (1666)<br>**War of Devolution** begins as French invade Netherlands (1667-8)<br>**Peace of Breda (1667)**<br>**Venice** loses Crete to Turks (1669)<br>**Hudson's Bay Company** chartered (1670)<br>**Dodo** becomes extinct (c.1680) |
| **1681-1695** | **Telemann** b. (1681)<br>**Rameau** b. (1683)<br>**Bach** b. (1685)<br>**Handel** b. (1685)<br>**First English opera** produced: Purcell's *Dido and Aeneas* (c. 1689)<br>**Purcell** *The Indian Queen,* London (1695)<br>**Purcell** d. (1695) | **Turks** besiege Vienna (1683)<br>**Louis XIV** moves court to Versailles (1682<br>**Edict of Nantes** revoked (1685)<br>**Chinese** ports open to foreign trade (1685<br>**James II** expelled (1688); William and Ma begin joint reign (1689)<br>**Smyrna** destroyed by an earthquake (1688<br>**Bank of England** founded (1694) |
| **1696-1710** | **String orchestras** established (c. 1700)<br>**Horn** first used in orchestra (c. 1700)<br>**Pachelbel** d. (1706)<br>**Silbermann** builds his first organ (1707)<br>**Cristofori** of Florence produces first piano (1709)<br>**Handel** becomes Kapellmeister to Elector of Hanover (1710) | **Peter the Great** in Western Europe (1697)<br>**Peace of Karlowitz** (1699)<br>**Electorate of Brandenburg** becomes Kingdom of Prussia (1701)<br>**War of the Spanish Succession** (1702-13)<br>**Foundations of St Petersburg** laid (1703)<br>**Battle of Blenheim** (1704)<br>**England and Scotland** are united (1707) |
| **1711-1725** | **Corelli** 12 *Concerti Grossi* (1712)<br>**Handel** *Water Music* (1714)<br>**Vivaldi** *Four Seasons* (1716)<br>**Bach** *G minor Fantasia and Fugue* (c. 1717-23)<br>**Clarinet** first used in orchestra (c. 1720)<br>**Bach** Brandenburg Concertos (1721)<br>**J.J. Fux** *Gradus ad Parnassum,* treatise on counterpoint (1725) | **Peace of Adrianople** (1713)<br>**Queen Anne** d.; George I begins reign (17<br>**Louis XIV** d.; accession of Louis XV as a minor (1715)<br>**Battle of Preston** (1715)<br>**Treaty of Passarowitz** (1718)<br>**Pragmatic Sanction** establishes indivisibil of Austria-Hungary (1720) |
| **1726-1740** | **Handel** becomes British subject (1726)<br>**John Gay** *Beggar's Opera* (1728)<br>**Rameau** *La Poule* (1728)<br>**Bach** *St Matthew Passion* (1729)<br>**Covent Garden Opera House** opened (1732)<br>**Haydn** b. (1732)<br>**J.C. Bach**, Bach's youngest son, b. (1735)<br>**Haydn** joins Vienna court chapel choir (1740) | **Anglo-Spanish War** (1727-8) confirms Britis possession of Gibraltar<br>**Coffee** first planted in Brazil (1727)<br>**Excavation of Herculaneum** begins (1738)<br>**Treaty of Belgrade** (1739)<br>**War of Jenkins's Ear** (1739-41)<br>**Frederick the Great** makes first move in the War of the Austrian Succession (1740-8) |
| **1741-1755** | **Vivaldi** d. (1741)<br>**John Wesley** publishes first Methodist hymn tunes (1742)<br>**Handel** *Messiah* (1742)<br>**Handel** *Firework Music* (1749)<br>**Bach** Art of Fugue (1749)<br>**Bach** d. (1750)<br>**Albinoni** d. (1751) | **Battle of Fontenoy** (1745)<br>**Battle of Culloden** (1746)<br>**Revolution** in Holland (1747)<br>**Treaty of Aix-la-Chapelle** ends War of the Austrian Succession (1748)<br>**Pompeii** is found (1748)<br>**Moscow University** founded (1755)<br>**Lisbon** destroyed by an earthquake (1755) |
| **1756-1770** | **Mozart** b. (1756)<br>**Handel** d. (1759)<br>**Gluck** *Orpheus and Euridice,* Vienna (1762)<br>**Mozart** starts tours as child prodigy (1763)<br>**Rameau** d. (1764)<br>**J.C. Bach** piano recitals, London (1764)<br>**Telemann** d. (1767)<br>**Beethoven** b. (1770) | **Casanova** escapes from Venice prison (175<br>**George III** begins reign (1760)<br>**Catherine the Great** takes power (1762)<br>**Seven Years War** ends; British power in India and Canada is confirmed (1763)<br>**Potatoes** introduced into Europe (c.1765)<br>**Corsica** ceded to France (1768)<br>**Tennessee** is settled by Europeans (1769) |
| **1771-1785** | **Waltz** becomes popular in Vienna (1773)<br>**Charles Burney** *A General History of Music* (1776)<br>**Ancient Music** Concerts sponsored by George III (1776-89)<br>**Mozart** *Flute and Harp Concerto,* Paris (1778)<br>**Broadwood** patents piano pedal (1783)<br>**Mozart** *Piano Concertos,* K.467, K.482 (1785) | **First partition** of Poland (1772)<br>**Boston Tea Party** (1773)<br>**Louis XV** d.; accession of Louis XVI (1774)<br>**American War of Independence** (1775-83)<br>**Gordon Riots** in London (1780)<br>**Industrial Revolution** underway with growth of English cotton industry (after 1780)<br>**Potemkin** conquers Crimea for Russia (1783 |
| **1786-1800** | **Mozart** *Don Giovanni* (1787)<br>**Mozart** *Eine Kleine Nachtmusik* (1787)<br>**Mozart** *Symphonies nos. 40 and 41* (1788)<br>**Mozart** *Clarinet Concerto* (1789)<br>**Mozart** d. (1791)<br>**Haydn** *Symphonies nos. 94 and 101* (1791-4)<br>**Rouget de Lisle** *La Marseillaise* (1792)<br>**Beethoven** *Symphony no. 1* (1799) | **Frederick the Great** d. (1786)<br>**Convicts** settled in Australia (1788)<br>**American Constitution** signed (1787) Washington elected President (1789)<br>**French Revolution** begins (1789)<br>**Louis XVI** executed; Reign of Terror (1793)<br>**Rosetta Stone** is found (1799)<br>**Britain and Ireland** united (1800) |

## IE ARTS

cartes d. (1650)
bes *Leviathan* (1651)
romini & Ramaldi begin St Agnes, Rome (1652)
asquez *Las Meninas* (1656)
nini begins St Peter's Piazza (1656)
ys begins *Diary* (1660)
meer *The Lacemaker* (1664)
nbrandt *The Jewish Bride* (1665)

ière *Le Misanthrope* (1666)
ton *Paradise Lost* (1667)
sailles remodelled by Le Vau (1669)
noza *Tractatus Theologico-politicus* (1670)
cal *Pensées* (1670)
rquise de Sévigné begins famous letters (1671)
en begins St Paul's Cathedral (1675)
yan *Pilgrim's Progress* (1678)

Brun *Salon de la Guerre,* Versailles (1686)
ke *On Civil Government* (1689)
bema *The Avenue, Middelharnis* (1689)
ing *Esther* (1689)
her von Erlach begins Schönbrunn (c. 1691)
zo ceiling of St Ignazio, Rome (1691-4)
tionnaire de L'Académie Française (1694)
den *Love Triumphant* (1694)

demy of Arts founded, Berlin (1696)
rault collection of fairy tales (1697)
itehall Palace burnt down (1697)
t English daily newspaper *The Daily Courant* (1702)
nheim Palace built by Vanbrugh (1705)
rnhill creates Painted Hall, Greenwich (1707)
ele launches *Tatler* (1709)
t English copyright act in force (1710)

dison founds *The Spectator* (1711)
e *Rape of the Lock* (1714)
polo *Sacrifice of Isaac* (1715)
tteau *Departure from the Isle of Cythera* (1717)
oe *Robinson Crusoe* (1719)
erbrandt designs Vienna's Belvedere (1720-4)
ntesquieu *Lettres Persanes* (1721)
lington and Kent build Chiswick House (1725)

ft *Gulliver's Travels* (1726)
vi builds Trevi Fountain, Rome (1726-8)
nolds *Three Ladies Adorning a Term of Hymen* (1733)
arth completes *Rake's Progress* (1735)
rdin *Saying Grace* (1739)
ne *Treatise on Human Nature* (1739-40)
ardson *Pamela* (1740)
aletto *St Mark's Square* (1740)

rick's theatrical début in London (1741)
ghi *The Apothecary's Shop* (1741)
ding *Tom Jones* (1749)
pole designs Strawberry Hill (1750)
erot *Encyclopédie* Vol. 1 (1751)
cher *The Judgement of Paris* (1754)
ppendale *Gentleman and Cabinetmaker's Directory* (1754)

nesi *Antichità Romana* (1757)
taire *Candide* (1759)
ne *Tristram Shandy* (1759-67)
sseau *The Social Contract* (1762)
ckelmann *History of Ancient Art* 1763-4
onard *The Swing* (1766)
al Academy founded (1768)
dgwood factory, Etruria, founded (1769)

nsborough *Blue Boy* (c.1771)
rm und Drang manifesto (1773)
th *The Wealth of Nations* (1776)
bon *Decline and Fall of the Roman Empire* (1776)
erial Ballet School, St Petersburg, founded (1779)
iller *Die Räuber* (1781)
t *Critique of Pure Reason* (1781)
id *Oath of the Horatii* (1785)

ke *Songs of Innocence* (1789)
ke *Reflections on the Revolution in France* (1790)
well *Life of Johnson* (1791)
e *Rights of Man* (1791)
llstonecraft *Vindication of the Rights of Women* (1792)
man illustrations to *Iliad* and *Odyssey* (1793)
a *Los Caprichos* (1799)

## SCIENCE

**Air pump** invented by Guericke (c.1650)
**Pendulum clock** invented by Huygens (1657)
**Glauber** *De Natura Salium* (1658)
**Royal Society** founded (1660)
**Malpighi** completes Harvey's theory on blood circulation (1661)
**Newton** conceives theory of gravity (1664-6)
**Hooke** finds living cells in plants (1665)

**Académie Royale des Sciences** founded (1666)
**Spectrum** discovered by Newton (1666)
**Steno** begins modern geology (1669)
**Leibniz** defines existence of the ether (1671)
**Greenwich Observatory** founded (1675)
**Speed of light** calculated by Roemer (1675)
**Protozoa** discovered by Leeuwenhoek (1677)
**Niagara Falls** discovered by Hannepin (1679)

**Mississippi** explored by La Salle (1681)
**Halley** observes comet (1682)
**Bacteria** drawn by Leeuwenhoek (1683)
**Efficiency force-pump** designed by Perrault (1684)
**Newton** *Philosophiae Naturalis Principia Mathematicia,* basis of modern maths (1687)
**Wave theory of light** presented by Huygens (1690)
**Plant sexes** explained by Camerarius (1694)

**Savery** makes practical steam engine (1696)
**Speed of sound** calculated by Newton (1698)
**North-west Australia** explored by Dampier (1699)
**Berlin Academy of Science** founded (1700)
**Newton** *Optics* (1704)
**Steam engine** improved by Newcomen (1704)
**China** is mapped by Jesuits (1708)
**Coke-blast iron** produced by Darby (1709)

**First mine ventilator** made by Partels (1711)
**Eustachio's** anatomical works published (1714)
**Fahrenheit** invents mercury thermometer (1714)
**Fine-pointed surgical syringe** invented by Anel (1714)
**Iron ramrod** invented by Leopold of Dessau (1718)
**Halley** discovers true motion of fixed stars (1718)
**St Petersburg Academy of Science** founded by Catherine the Great (1725)

**Hale** *Vegetable Staticks* (1727)
**Bering** discovers Straits (1728)
**Cobalt** isolated by Brandt (1730)
**Boerhaave** *Elements of Chemistry* (1732)
**Linnaeus** begins *Systema Naturae* (1735)
**Harrison's** first marine chronometer (1735)
**Euler** *Mechanica* (1736)
**Swedish Scientific Academy** founded (1739)

**Anson** sets out on voyage round the world (1740)
**Celsius** invents centigrade thermometer (1742)
**D'Alembert** *Traité de Dynamique* (1743)
**Leyden jar** invented by Kleist (1745)
**Buffon** *Histoire Naturelle* Vol. I (1749)
**Franklin** invents lightning conductor (1752)
**Carbon dioxide** identified by Black (1754)
**Electroscope** invented by Canton (1754)

**Venus atmosphere** discovered by Lomonosov (1761)
**Hydrogen** identified by Cavendish (1766)
**Bougainville** starts voyage to Pacific (1766)
**Watt** patents steam engine (1769)
**Cook** begins first voyage to the Antipodes (1768)
**Hargreave's** spinning jenny (1767)
**Priestley** *History and Present State of Electricity* (1767)

**Galvani** discovers electric nature of nervous impulse (1771)
**Crompton's** spinning mule (1773)
**Lavoisier** shows that air consists mainly of hydrogen and oxygen (1774)
**Hawaii** discovered by Cook (1778)
**Uranus** discovered by Herschel (1781)
**First human flight** in hot-air balloon (1783)

**Uranium** discovered by Klaproth (1786)
**Linnean** Society founded (1788)
**Soda-making process** developed by Leblanc (1791)
**Coal-gas** produced by Murdoch (1792)
**Pollination** process discovered by Sprengel (1793)
**Rumford** discovers nature of heat or kinetic energy (1798)
**Volta** invents battery (1800)

*Purcell*

*Vivaldi*

*Rameau*

*Handel*

*Mozart*

*Denis Diderot (right). With d'Alembert he masterminded France's* Encylopédie, *the means by which the most advanced ideas of the 18th century were disseminated. A massive project, the work occupied 15 years of Diderot's life. For much of that time he had to struggle alone aainst religious and political opposition.*

Louvre/Scala

Mauro Pucciarelli

*The New Zealander (above), who was encountered and painted on a Captain Cook voyage, has been idealized as a 'noble savage'. Man 'in a state of nature' was believed to be pure.*

## The Enlightenment

During the Enlightenment, which is reckoned to have been at its peak from about 1740 to 1765, Europe's attention was focused on Paris, the capital of culture. Ever since the reign of Louis XIV at his fabulous base in Versailles, France had set the pace for refinement of behaviour and everything to do with taste: furniture, clothes and *haute cuisine*. But with the Enlightenment this interest in all things French became even more pronounced.

Every educated person learned French, which had replaced Latin as Europe's common language, and everything published in French was accessible to the whole of polite society. Anyone who could afford it employed a French cook, and French fashions were avidly followed. (In fact music was the only branch of the arts in which fashionable society accepted German talent as superior to the French.)

But the true *douceur de vivre* (sweetness of living) could be enjoyed most in Paris, where the salons run by cultivated women enabled intellectuals to socialize and speculate at the same time.

## The Encyclopédie

Denis Diderot was a many-sided *salonier* of genius and the great project he dedicated most of his life to, the *Encyclopédie (Dictionnaire Raisonné des Sciences, des Arts et des Métiers),* is often regarded as typifying the attitude of the Enlightenment. It was an immense compendium of knowledge, comprising 17 volumes of text and seven of plates. The *Encyclopédie* was intended to be an anthology of the very latest technological information, which by being published could be disseminated and serve as the basis for further advances in science and technology. It was an attempt to substitute real knowledge and know-how for traditional beliefs, and whatever was 'scientific', whatever helped individuals to achieve self-awareness, was suitable for inclusion.

Accordingly, along with treatises on the latest inventions, the *Encyclopédie* included 'enlightened' opinions on politics, philosophy and religion, Diderot himself, the dynamo behind the whole project (which incidentally, was a great publishing

Jacques Lajoue 'Le Cabinet Physique de M. Bonnier de la Mosson'. The Beit Collection, Russborough, Ireland

success), reflected his wide and enlightened range of interests by contributing articles on topics ranging from Aristotle to artificial flowers.

Of course, only a tiny minority read the *Encylopédie* and few people followed in detail the intense intellectual debates being carried on in the coffee houses and salons of Paris, London and Amsterdam. The 18th century was also the period of sexually adventurous 'libertines' such as Casanova and gossip-loving socialites who saw social polish as an end in itself. But this good-time scene was also a part of the Enlightenment, which was basically an optimistic, curious and celebratory state of mind. Instead of being a 'vale of tears', the world was made for man's delight: eager theorists suggested that the

Rococo artists aimed to delight their audiences rather than overwhelm or exalt them as the Baroque painters had done.

But even though the Enlightenment mood could sometimes be superficially optimistic – peasants only felt its benefits to the extent that their enlightened social superiors felt benevolent towards them – its concrete results were significant. Partly because of a new intolerance of blind cruelty it was in the 18th century that witchcraft trials either came to a spontaneous end or were declared illegal in one country after another. And whereas religious feeling had supplied the Baroque spirit with its serious dimension, the Enlightenment derived much of its inspiration from the classical civilizations of Greece and Rome.

### Classicism

The 18th century saw a great revival of direct interest – previously the classics had been largely mediated by the church – in the glory that was Greece and the grandeur that was Rome. The stoic morality of republican Rome appealed particularly to an age in which new secular values were being sought, while the 'purity' and simplicity of Greek and Roman architecture, which was being excavated and restored in the 18th century, found ready admirers and imitators. In understanding Classicism in music it helps that, like the Baroque, there was a recognizable artistic 'climate', for it was during the Enlightenment that the disciplined and balanced forms of classical thought came to terms with new ideas about free individual expression. In the words of one historian of music (P. H. Lang),

*Classicism beautified life . . . its principal object was man living in consort with nature, man beautiful in body and soul, in bearing and in deed, man who became aware of his own living harmony, and who was the measure of all things.*

*This painting shows part of the collection of a rich 18th-century dilettante (far left). The objects on display reveal the range of such an 'enlightened' gentleman's interests. They include optical instruments and lenses, crystals and mechanical models of cranes and waterwheels, as well as sculptures, and all are housed in a lavishly decorated setting.*

*Charles Towneley, who had one of the best collections of classical antiquities in the world, gathers with other English connoisseurs in his library (below). After his death in 1805 Towneley's collection was purchased by the British Museum, which had been founded in 1759.*

watermelon was shaped precisely so that it could be sliced easily, that the density of water was designed to facilitate navigation, and so on. There was a tremendous excitement in the air as exotic lands were 'discovered' by Europeans and new foods such as coffee and the potato spread into the cuisines of Europe.

The art that complemented this aspect of the Enlightenment is called 'Rococo' – from the French *style rocaille*, a free-flowing style of shell and scrollwork that was entirely decorative and charming. In their paintings Rococo masters such as Watteau celebrated elegance rather than grandeur and when they did treat religious topics it was with grace and sentiment rather than solemn conviction.

Johann Zoffany 'Charles Towneley in his Gallery' Towneley Hall Art Gallery/Burnley Borough Council

# The Romantic era
## 1800-1890

*The composers of the Romantic era were caught up in an electric atmosphere of revolution and protest. New ideals of freedom and individualism took Europe by storm, and fired the imagination of great artists like Beethoven.*

*Portrayed here by the painter Caspar David Friedrich is the archetypal Romantic figure,* The Wanderer Above a Sea of Mist. *He stands at one with the forces of Nature and alone in a world of conflict – contemplative, pessimistic, tormented and passionate. It could almost be a view of Beethoven himself.*

e term 'Romantic' is one of the great labels of story, a label that was, and still is, applied so loosely at it is hard to believe that what began as a great and nscious intellectual revolution has degenerated o a byword for sentimentality, frills and rather ndless, if pretty, self-indulgence. To understand at the poets, painters, composers and political ilosophers and activists of the late 18th and 19th nturies meant by this label, the preceding age of lightenment has to be confronted. The Romantics re history's first 'angry young men'. They were acting against the old world as much as they were ponding to the new. The whole process can even imagined as something very familiar: the neration gap.

A true representative of the Enlightenment believed the power of reason. The world was a product of a per rationality, that of God, who was worshipped as divine orchestrator of a 'Grand Scheme'. The iverse 'worked' according to rules which, once derstood, could be interpreted for the greater lfare of humanity. An Enlightenment garden, for ample, might contain beautifully controlled plants,

Mary Evans Picture Library

*Marat (above), the 'Friend of the People', helped to inspire the overthrow of the French monarchy. The spirit of the revolution is epitomized by Delacroix's painting of* **Liberty Leading the People** *(below) – a powerful testament to the era's thirst for freedom.*

a formal, ordered arrangement of nature. So progressive farmers could 'improve' the landscape to yield bigger crops and fatter animals, and capitalists could 'rationalize' working processes and harness new materials and new technology to yield profit. Everything pointed towards progress; if any mystery remained that was only because no one had yet worked out the rules. The Enlightenment celebrated an ongoing status quo.

But the individuals who described themselves as Romantic, and individuals they most emphatically were, saw things, felt things, in a very different way. Their garden was a wonderfully wild, colourful and profuse environment, a source of inspiration. Artists – be they painters, poets or musicians – had a duty to respond to beauty and to the most rousing events of the age. The material progress facilitated by the Enlightenment had to be accompanied by political and spiritual liberation, and so the Romantics thrilled to the first stirrings of democratic revolution in Europe. Instead of the 'mob' they saw the 'people' rising; instead of being a coldly calculated struggle for survival, life was full of promise and hope.

Louvre/Bridgeman Art Library

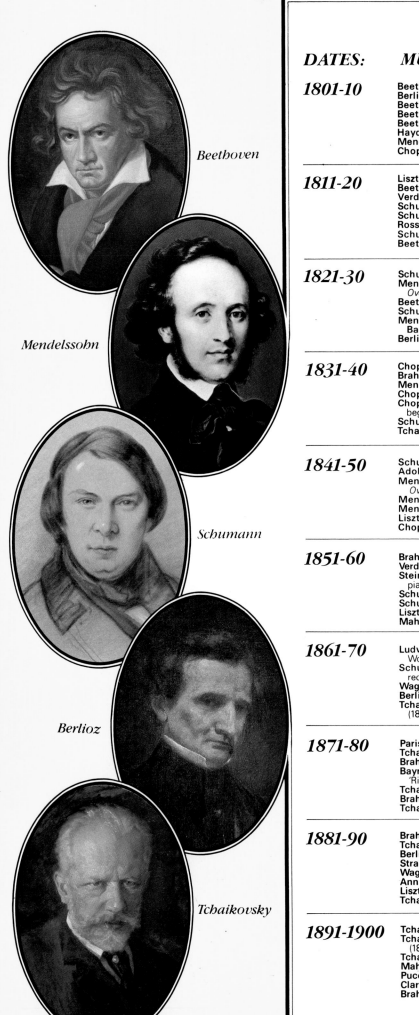

*Beethoven*

*Mendelssohn*

*Schumann*

*Berlioz*

*Tchaikovsky*

| DATES: | MUSIC | HISTORY |
|---|---|---|
| **1801-10** | Beethoven *Piano Sonatas* (1801/1804)<br>Berlioz b. (1803)<br>Beethoven *Violin Concerto* (1806)<br>Beethoven *Symphony no. 5* (1808)<br>Beethoven *'Emperor' Concerto* (1809)<br>Haydn d. (1809)<br>Mendelssohn b. (1809)<br>Chopin and Schumann b. (1810) | T. Jefferson becomes US President (180...<br>Napoleon proclaimed Emperor (1804)<br>Battle of Trafalgar (1805)<br>Holy Roman Empire ends (1806)<br>Slave Trade abolished in Britain (1807)<br>Peninsular War in Spain (1808)<br>Metternich becomes chief minister of<br>Austria (1809) |
| **1811-20** | Liszt b. (1811)<br>Beethoven meets Goethe (1812)<br>Verdi and Wagner b. (1813)<br>Schubert begins writing songs (1814)<br>Schubert *Symphony no. 5* (1816)<br>Rossini 'Barber of Seville' (1816)<br>Schubert *'Trout' Quintet* (1819)<br>Beethoven goes deaf (1819) | George III pronounced insane (1811)<br>Napoleon's retreat from Moscow (1812)<br>Jews in Russia emancipated (1812)<br>Napoleon banished to Elba (1814)<br>Battle of Waterloo (1815)<br>Congress of Vienna set up (1814-15)<br>Victoria and Albert b. (1819)<br>George III d. succeeded by George IV (182... |
| **1821-30** | Schubert *'Unfinished' Symphony* (1822)<br>Mendelssohn *'Midsummer Night's Dream'*<br>*Overture* (1826)<br>Beethoven d. (1827)<br>Schubert d. (1828)<br>Mendelssohn rediscovers and revives<br>Bach's 'St. Matthew's Passion' (1829)<br>Berlioz *Symphonie Fantastique* (1830) | Napoleon d. (1821)<br>Greek War of Independence (1822)<br>Simon Bolivar leads revolution in Latin<br>America (1822)<br>Decembrist revolt in Russia (1825)<br>Turkey recognises Greek Independence<br>(1829)<br>Revolution in Paris (1830) |
| **1831-40** | Chopin arrives in Paris (1831)<br>Brahms b. (1833)<br>Mendelssohn *'Italian' Symphony* (1833)<br>Chopin *12 Etudes, op. 10* (1833)<br>Chopin's relationship with George Sands<br>begins (1838)<br>Schumann marries Clara (1840)<br>Tchaikovsky b. (1840) | 'Italian Youth' movement launched by<br>Giuseppe Mazzini (1831)<br>Spanish Inquisition suppressed (1834)<br>Davy Crockett killed at the Alamo (1836...<br>Victoria becomes Queen of England (183...<br>First Opium War (1839)<br>Queen Victoria marries Prince Albert<br>(1840) |
| **1841-50** | Schumann *'Spring' Symphony* (1841)<br>Adolphe Sax invents the saxophone (1841)<br>Mendelssohn's *'Midsummer Night's Dream*<br>*Overture'* premièred (1843)<br>Mendelssohn *Violin Concerto* (1844)<br>Mendelssohn d. (1847)<br>Liszt's first Symphonic Poem (1848-9)<br>Chopin d. (1849) | British Hong Kong sovereignty (1841)<br>US war with Mexico begins (1846)<br>Corn Laws repealed by Parliament (1846...<br>Potato famine in Ireland (1846-8)<br>California Gold Rush (1847)<br>Communist manifesto issued by Marx<br>and Engels (1848)<br>Revolutions throughout Europe (1848) |
| **1851-60** | Brahms tours with Reményi (1852)<br>Verdi 'La Traviata', Venice (1853)<br>Steinway sets up his New York firm of<br>piano manufacturers (1853)<br>Schumann attempts suicide (1854)<br>Schumann d. (1856)<br>Liszt *Piano Concerti nos. 1 and 2* (late 1850s)<br>Mahler b. (1860) | Louis Napoleon proclaimed Napoleon I...<br>restores French Empire (1852)<br>The Crimean War (1854-6)<br>Serbia's independence recognised by<br>Europe (1856)<br>Indian Mutiny (1857)<br>British Rule in India transferred to the<br>Crown (1858) |
| **1861-70** | Ludwig Köchel 'Catalogue of Mozart's<br>Works' (1862)<br>Schubert's *'Unfinished' Symphony*<br>rediscovered and premièred (1865)<br>Wagner 'Tristan und Isolde' (1865)<br>Berlioz d. (1869)<br>Tchaikovsky *'Romeo and Juliet' Overture*<br>(1870) | Unification of Italy (1861)<br>American Civil War (1861)<br>Emancipation of Russian serfs (1861)<br>Bismarck becomes Prussian PM (1862)<br>Slavery abolished in US (1865)<br>Marx 'Das Kapital' Vol. 1 (1867)<br>Suez Canal opened (1869)<br>Franco-Prussian War (1870) |
| **1871-80** | Paris Opéra completed (1874)<br>Tchaikovsky *Piano Concerto no. 1* (1875)<br>Brahms *Symphony no. 1* (1876)<br>Bayreuth Festival opens with Wagner's<br>'Ring' cycle (1876)<br>Tchaikovsky *Swan Lake* (1877)<br>Brahms *Violin Concerto* (1878)<br>Tchaikovsky *'1812' Overture* (1880) | Paris Commune set up (1871)<br>Pope allowed possession of the Vatican<br>(1871)<br>Spanish Civil War (1872)<br>Disraeli becomes British PM (1874)<br>Victoria becomes Empress of India (187...<br>Stalin and Trotsky b. (1879)<br>British Zulu War (1879) |
| **1881-90** | Brahms *Piano Concerto no. 2* (1881)<br>Tchaikovsky *Capriccio Italien* (1881)<br>Berlin Philharmonic founded (1882)<br>Stravinsky b. (1882)<br>Wagner d. (1883)<br>Anna Pavlova b. (1885)<br>Liszt d. (1886)<br>Tchaikovsky *Sleeping Beauty* (1889) | Jews persecuted in Russia (1881)<br>Triple Alliance between Austria, Germa...<br>and Italy formed (1882)<br>General Gordon killed at Khartoum (188...<br>Gladstone brings in bill for Home Rule in<br>Ireland (1886)<br>Adolf Hitler b. (1889)<br>Bismarck dismissed by William II (1890) |
| **1891-1900** | Tchaikovsky *Nutcracker* (1892)<br>Tchaikovsky *Symphony no. 6 'Pathétique'*<br>(1893)<br>Tchaikovsky d. (1893)<br>Mahler *Symphony no. 3* (1893-6)<br>Puccini 'La Bohème', Turin (1896)<br>Clara Schumann d. (1896)<br>Brahms d. (1897) | Independent Labour Party formed (189...<br>British South Africa Company territory<br>becomes Rhodesia (1895)<br>First Olympics held in Athens (1896)<br>Victoria's Diamond Jubilee (1897)<br>Dreyfus forgery trial: Zola's letter to<br>French President 'J'accuse' (1898)<br>The Boer War (1899) |

# OMANTIC ERA

## THE ARTS

hateaubriand 'Atala' (1801)
me de Staël 'Delphine' (1802)
rner 'Shipwreck' (1805)
egel 'Phenomenology of the Mind' (1807)
gres begins 'La Source' (1807)
oethe 'Faust' Part I (1808)
riedrich 'The Cross in the Mountains' (1808)
erman Nazarenes founded (1809)

rothers Grimm 'Fairy Tales' (1812)
lgin Marbles brought to England (1812)
yron begins 'Childe Harold's Pilgrimage' (1812)
cott 'Waverley' (1814)
oya 'The Third of May 1808' (1814)
oleridge 'Sybilline Leaves' (1816)
ericault 'Raft of the Medusa' (1819)
helley 'Prometheus Unbound' (1820)

onstable 'Haywain' (1821)
homas de Quincy 'Confessions of an English
Opium Eater' (1821)
ushkin 'Eugene Onegin' (1822)
elacroix 'Massacre at Chios' (1824)
ebas begins building Notre Dame (1823)
anzoni 'I Promessi Sposi' (1825)
tendhal 'Le Rouge et le Noir' (1830)

ictor Hugo 'Notre Dame' (1831)
oethe 'Faust' Part II (1832)
chlegel completes his German Shakespeare
translation (1833)
eorge Sand 'Lélia' (1833)
okusai '36 views of Mount Fuji' (1834-5)
oe 'The Fall of the House of Usher' (1839)
ermentov 'A Hero of our Times' (1840)

ogol's 'Dead Souls' published (first part) (1842)
Vordsworth becomes Poet Laureate (1843)
uskin 'Modern Painters' Vol. 1 (1843)
rner 'Rain, Steam and Speed' (1844)
Bronte 'Wuthering Heights' (1847)
re-Raphaelite Brotherhood founded (1848)
Murger 'Scènes de la vie de Bohème' (1848)
ourbet 'The Stonebreakers' (1850)

he Great Exhibition in London (1851)
ongfellow 'The Song of Hiawatha' (1855)
Valt Whitman 'Leaves of Grass' (1855)
audelaire 'Les Fleurs du Mal' (1857)
Fitzgerald 'Rubáiyát of Omar Kayyám' (1859)
rts and Crafts movement set up (late 1850s)
urckhardt 'The Civilisation of the Renaissance in
Italy' (1860)

urgenev 'Fathers and Sons' (1862)
anet 'Déjeuner sur l'herbe' (1863)
olstoy 'War and Peace' (1864)
ickens 'Our Mutual Friend' (1864)
winburne 'Atlanta in Calydon' (1865)
ostoevsky 'Crime and Punishment' (1866)
aris World's Fair exhibits Japanese art (1867)
aubert 'L'education Sentimentale' (1869)

. Eliot 'Middlemarch' (1871)
irst Impressionist Exhibition, Paris (1874)
erlaine 'Romance sans parole' (1874)
enoir 'Le Moulin de la Galette' (1876)
1. Twain 'Tom Sawyer' (1876)
Vhistler vs. Ruskin libel action (1878)
ola 'Nana' (1880)
odin 'The Thinker' (1880)

icasso b. (1881)
. L. Stevenson 'Treasure Island' (1882)
ietzsche 'Thus Spake Zarathustra' (1883)
eurat 'Bathers' (1884)
an Gogh 'The Potato Eaters' (1885)
ézanne 'Mont Sainte-Victoire' (1885)
scar Wilde 'The Picture of Dorian Gray' (1890)
sen 'Hedda Gabler' (1890)

homas Hardy 'Tess of the D'Urbervilles' (1891)
uluose Lautrec 'Moulin Rouge' (1892)
rt Nouveau style emerges (1893)
enkiewicz 'Quo Vadis' (1895)
V. B. Yeats 'Poems' (1895)
. G. Wells 'The War of the Worlds' (1898)
hekhov 'Uncle Vanya' (1900)
eud 'The Interpretation of Dreams' (1900)

## SCIENCE

The first submarine , 'Nautilus', produced by Robert
Fulton (1801)
Ultra violet light discovered in the sun's spectrum by
Johann Ritter (1801)
Shell invented by Henry Shrapnel (1803)
Fulton's steamship makes its first voyage (1807)
River Ganges' source is discovered (1808)
Canning food techniques developed by Appet (1810)

Machine for spinning flax invented by Girard (1812)
First steam locomotive constructed by George
Stephenson (1814)
Miner's safety lamp invented by Humphry Davy
(1815)
Stethoscope invented by R. T. Laënnec (1816)
Detector lock invented by Jeremiah Chubb (1818)
Electromagnetism discovered by Oersted (1820)

Egyptian hieroglyphics deciphered by Champollion,
using Rosetta Stone (1821)
Principle of electric dynamo discovered by Faraday
(1821)
Waterproof fabric invented by Charles Macintosh
(1823)
Stockton-Darlington railroad opens (1825)
Photographs produced by Niepce (1827)

Charles Darwin sails on HMS Beagle (1831)
Principle of modern computer developed by
Charles Babbage (1834)
Colt patents his single barrel pistol (1835)
Morse Code invented by Samuel Morse (1837)
Daguerre and Niepce present their method of
photography (1838)
Vulcanization is discovered by C. Goodyear (1839)

Hypnosis discovered by James Braid (1841)
Standard screw threads proposed by Whitworth
(1841)
Wood-pulp paper invented by F. G. Keller (1844)
Ether as an anaesthetic used by W. T. Morton (1846)
Nitroglycerine discovered by Ascanio Sobrero (1846)
Rotary printing press invented by Richard Hoe (1847)
Bunsen burner produced by R. W. Bunsen (1850)

Sewing machine developed by Isaac Singer (1851)
Rotation of the earth proved by Jean Foucault (1851)
Livingstone discovers the Victoria Falls (1855)
Converter for steel-making process introduced by
Henry Bessemer (1856)
Charles Darwin 'On the Origin of Species' puts
forward the theory of evolution (1859)
First oil well drilled (1859), in Pennsylvania

Speed of light measured by Lion Foucault (1862)
First underground railway opened in London (1863)
Pasteurization invented by Louis Pasteur (1864)
Genetics experiments published by G. Mendel (1865)
Antiseptic surgery introduced by Lord Lister (1865)
Dynamite invented by Alfred Nobel (who established
the Nobel prize) (1866)
Typewriter invented by Christopher Sholes (1867)

Typewriter developed commercially (1870s)
Oceanography founded by the Challenger expedition
(1872-6)
Telephone invented by A. Graham Bell (1876)
Bacteria identified by Robert Koch (1876)
Phonograph invented by Thomas Edison (1877)
Microphone invented by David Hughes (1878)
Electric light bulb patented by Edison (1879)

Natural History Museum opened (1881)
Fingerprints proved to be individual by Sir F. Galton
(1885)
Motor car invented by Karl Benz (1885)
Radio waves produced by Heinrich Hertz (1887)
Celluloid film invented by H.W. Goodwin (1887)
Photographic film developed by G. Eastman (1888)
Pneumatic tyre invented by John Dunlop (1888)

Diesel engine patented by Rudolf Diesel (1892)
Henry Ford builds his first car (1893)
Radio telegraphy invented by Marconi (1895)
X-rays discovered by Roentgen (1895)
Safety razor invented by Gillette (1895)
Motion picture invented by Edison (1896)
Pavlov's first experiment with conditioned reflexes
(1900)

Schubert

Chopin

Liszt

Brahms

Mahler

Pictures supplied by Archiv für Kunst und Geschichte, Bildarchiv, Preussischer Kulturbesitz, Bulloz, Edimedia, Louvre/Giraudon, Mansell Collection, Salmer

*This early watercolour by Turner of Tintern Abbey (right) demonstrates the attraction of Gothic architecture for Romantic artists. Along with other things medieval, it was felt to be one of the truest expressions of religious feeling. It was at Tintern Abbey that Wordsworth mused on 'the still, sad music of humanity'.*

*In an age of conflict, Goya's electrifying 3rd of May 1808 (below) gripped the Romantic imagination. It takes as its subject one of the atrocities that occurred following the French invasion of Spain. With almost savage pity, Goya highlights the plight of the Spanish people, pitting the individual – dressed in white – against a 'crowd' of faceless executioners.*

### The literary initiative

The Romantic movement was as international as it was inter-disciplinary – no art remained immune and every European culture added to its rich mix. It is fair to say, however, that literature took the initiative and that in the beginning German literature pioneered the whole trend. Ironically, Germany's cultural lead was partly due to her political and economic backwardness. While France was electrifying the world with revolutionary fervour, Britain was embarking on a career as the world's first great industrial power. But Germany – a collection of over 300 principalities and duchies – was only a cultural entity. German-speakers were looking for a compensatory literary identity, a hook upon which to hang their growing sense of nationhood, and Romanticism provided it.

The yearning for an alternative tradition was reflected in the extraordinary success of a literary fraud perpetrated by a Scottish poet, James Macpherson. In 1762 Macpherson began a cult that spread like wildfire throughout Europe when he published a selection of his 'translations' of the poetry of an ancient, semi-legendary Irish warrior-bard, Ossian. (Few people suspected that the so-called translations were in fact the inventions of Macpherson with little relation to genuine Gaelic lore.) The mystical Celtic world of Ossian, in combination with Scandinavian mythology and folklore, provided a new vein of literature to be tapped, beyond the monopoly of France, the traditional arbiter of good taste.

### ...mantic heroes

...the same time, the German 'high priest' of early ...manticism, Gotthold Lessing (1729–81), was ...smissing classical literary forms and recommending ...eturn to the values of Shakespeare and folk-songs ...cause of their lack of artificiality and their robust, ...rect appeal. Such preoccupations and theories ...vanced the *Sturm und Drang* ('storm and stress') ...ovement in Germany. The most notable member of ...is movement was Goethe (1749–1832), early ...omanticism's supreme literary hero.

...In *The Sorrows of Young Werther* (1774), a novel ...ritten in intense depression after an unhappy love ...air, Goethe caught the new mood perfectly with the ...le's alternation between great elation and intense ...elancholy. *Young Werther* tells the story of the love ...a gifted, sensitive young man for a woman already ...ppily betrothed to a decent, conventional and ...mpletely different kind of man. The sufferings of the ...ro are caused by love stifled by convention and the ...ner self destroyed by civilization, but pervading the ...ook is the understanding that absolute freedom is ...possible in an imperfect world. The combination of ...verse forces cripples Young Werther's will to live ...d Goethe's novel ends with his suicide. Soon after ...e book was published there followed a rash of ...icides – its readers identified with its hero and fell ...ctim to their own sensitivity. Goethe had written a ...anifesto against classicism, rationality and ...nvention, in the name of life, liberty, passion, nature

and youth. Young Werther's plight was all too appealing for a movement whose shock-troops were almost all young: the true Romantic dreaded the prospect of a respectable old age.

### The British contribution

In Britain a galaxy of poets – first Wordsworth and Coleridge, and then Byron, Shelley and Keats – represented and enhanced the Romantic focus on life. Wordsworth's and Coleridge's most famous literary collaboration, *Lyrical Ballads* (1798), was published against the backdrop of the recent French Revolution. Like most Romantics, the poets believed that they were witnessing the historic triumph of the free human spirit – 'Bliss was it in that dawn to be alive.' Wordsworth's strategy was to take 'ordinary things' and to show them in 'unusual aspect', believing that intense, almost religious joy could rise from a harmony with nature. Along with mysticism and political radicalism, a love of Nature was now a key ingredient in the Romantic consciousness.

The second generation of English Romantic poets – Byron, Shelley and Keats – explored different aspects of the Romantic experience. In their lives, as much as their work, these poets represented the rebellion against established society, the sense of longing, the fascination for the exotic and the heightened expression of emotion. It was said of the aristocratic, handsome Byron that he 'lost his native country and conquered Europe', so great was the impact of his

*The Romantic movement had an enduring obsession with the past – an obsession which was fed by the Scottish poet Macpherson when he published the alleged works of the Celtic warrior-bard Ossian. The impact of these ideas was immense, especially in Germany. Ossian is depicted (below) welcoming the ghosts of fallen heroes.*

poetry, which was set in Spain, Italy, the East and Greece. A fervent ally of the Greeks in the independence struggle against Turkey, he actually joined the revolt and died at Missolonghi in 1824.

### Romanticism and music

In essence, Romanticism in music involved the same ideals: the domination of feeling over order, instinct over reason; a fascination with the past mingled with ambitions for the future; a new preoccupation with nature (now considered wild and elemental rather than well-ordered and controlled) and a new concern with the importance of self-expression.

Thus, although it would be possible to apply the term 'Romantic' to the elements of music that were written before this period – in Bach's *Passions,* for example – effectively, the Romantic movement in music really began when composers, like artists, social reformers and philosophers, began to look to the imagination to express themselves rather than relying on faith or rational inquiry. Strangely enough, it took the musical world a while to catch up with the world of literature. The earliest moves towards Romanticism came almost a generation later in the works of Beethoven and Schubert. The emphasis passed from the dominating principles of classical proportions and reasoned progress – for example, the *sonata* form – to more dramatic expressions which were rather more dependent on the imagination. The flowering of opera during this period was due to this change of approach.

Naturally, instrumental music also developed new and flexible forms. Thus Beethoven, who was certainly a Romantic in his determination to use music as a moral force, wrote his Sixth Symphony ('Pastoral') to conjure up the countryside around Heiligenstadt – one of his favourite retreats outside Vienna; and his Third and Fifth Symphonies are powerful expressions of man struggling to assert his domination over the

*The English Romantic poet, Lord Byron, was an exotic hero who died fighting for the cause of Greek independence at Missolonghi.*

world – a basic Romantic ideal. Romantic symphonies and sonatas also tended to acquire titles – to emphasize connections with emotional states or a concealed 'programme' behind the music – hence 'Pastoral'. After Beethoven, music evolved still further along these lines. For example, Liszt was one of the first composers to write music that was not based merely on pure form, but on a fusion with a dramatic programme. He titled this innovative type of music a 'symphonic poem'.

Romanticism found its ultimate expression in the operas of Wagner. Unlike Beethoven, who had expressed generalized emotions through the symphonic form, Wagner put music at the service of drama, with music as the means and drama as the end. Inevitably, after the heights to which he had carried Romanticism in music, the movement went into decline.

The movement's practitioners themselves were not much help in defining Romanticism, because they used the term as a 'catch-all' slogan signifying a passionate reaction against the old order of fixed rules and forms. Despite these limitations, the term can be meaningfully applied to a composer like Beethoven, a painter like Goya and a poet like Goethe – they were all Romantics who pitted themselves against the 'middle ground' in life and the arts. In the wide sense in which it has been understood here, Romanticism was a self-conscious, militant trend in the arts, which dominated European culture from the French Revolution onwards. It is ironic, therefore, that by the late 19th century Romanticism had become the standard, 'respectable' creative approach.

*Blake's famous picture* **The Ancient of Days** *(right) sets the Creator in the swirling winds of chaos. Despite the mathematical dividers, the act of creation is clearly an exercise of divine will and inspiration. This visionary painting is a rejection of the 18th-century view of God as divine watchmaker.*

# *The Nationalist era*

## *1815-1914*

*During the 19th century, Europe underwent a radical change as popular movements sprang up in revolution against the 'old order'. And the expression of emerging national identities found voice in the music of the nationalist composers.*

The Romantic ideal continued to enthrall the hearts and minds of artists throughout the 19th century. But even as the Romantic flame burned its brightest, in the music of composers like Schumann, Chopin and Berlioz, so a new 'nationalist' ideal was kindled. From a few isolated sparks, Nationalism was fanned into a great movement that inspired some of the most beautiful of all compositions, and led music forward into the 20th century.

For almost a century the Romantic and Nationalist eras ran side by side and many Romantic and Nationalist artists lived through the same struggles, the same upheavals and the same remarkable events that transformed the world during the 19th century. Indeed, in many ways nationalism was a natural development of Romanticism and had much in common with it. But there was a crucial difference in attitude, a crucial difference in the response to those upheavals that set the Nationalists apart; they looked forward to the future while the Romantics gazed

*The boundaries of nations on the map of Europe in the 1860s (left) were startlingly different from the pattern familiar today. Many nations in eastern Europe were completely absorbed by the vast Russian, Austrian and Turkish empires, while Germany and Italy remained divided into numerous petty states and monarchies dominated by the might of Austria. No wonder, then, that nationalism became such a potent force in the revolutionary movements of 19th century Europe. By throwing off the yoke of imperial – and foreign – power nations became free to determine their own future prosperity.*

Bulloz

reaction to the social, religious and political straightjacket of the established order. But the assertive expression of national, rather than individual feeling was far more overtly political, and nationalist music is in many ways a form of protest, a call to arms in the cause of the country's freedom. No wonder then, that the nationalistic movement should be strongest in those countries where the jackboot of the ruling class trod heaviest.

Nationalism was very strong in Russia, a land where the Tsar ruled with a rod of iron, where serfdom was not abolished until 1861, where none but the aristocracy were free to move around the country and where the notorious 'Third Section' political police stamped out any protest. Here, a string of composers from Glinka to Mussorgsky took the often stirring, often hauntingly beautiful folk themes of their native land and added a new dimension to music. Novelists such as Tolstoy and Dostoyevsky created intense, overwhelming masterpieces that were uniquely Russian.

Individual nations swallowed by the vast Russian empire also struggled to find their own individual voice. Poland found Moniusko; the Finns rallied around the music of Sibelius.

In the countries under the yoke of the Habsburg Empire, where national identity was suppressed and the authorities spoke only in German, the nationalist strand was equally powerful. Bohemia (now Czechoslovakia), produced Smetana and Dvorák; in Hungary there was Erkel and later Bartok. Indeed, wherever there was oppression, a nationalist

Julian Falat 'Returning from a Bear Hunt'/Teresa Zoltowska

forever wistfully backwards.

The Romantics, with their colourful imaginative interpretation of life, had introduced the idea that music, and all art, could be a form of personal expression, not merely a craft. Yet, however rich and profuse was the variety of sources they drew their inspiration from, their music was essentially an expression of self, an expression of their own hopes and dreams, their own joys and their own struggles.

In contrast, the nationalist composers sought to express in their music national, rather than individual identity, with pride and love. In the process, of course, often an element of personality inevitably crept into the music – the warmth of Dvorák, the starkness of Mussorgsky and the sparkle of Rimsky-Korsakov is deeply personal. But the composer's love for his country remained the driving force.

Both Romanticism and Nationalism were revolutionary movements, reflecting the gathering

*The revolutionary slogan of the French insurgents of 1789 became the rallying cry for all those who fought to overthrow the old order (above).*
*While western Europe was becoming increasingly industrialized, the vast majority of people in the eastern areas remained tied to the land. It was to these stoical peasants, worn down by centuries of hardship, but remaining close to nature (right), that the nationalist composers looked for inspiration.*

*The July revolution in France in 1830 (right) was just one of the insurrections that convulsed Europe that year. In the same year, Belgium revolted against the Dutch and achieved independence, a Polish revolution was crushed brutally by the Russians and Spain embarked on a civil war that was to last ten years.*

composer stepped forward to speak up for his country. And the rich vein of music that they unlocked in the folk heritage of their countries provided a source of inspiration for composers the world over. Soon every composer began to look at the folk musical roots of his own country or, as in the case of Ravel, to the folk roots of other countries. Ravel, a Frenchman, found inspiration for his *Bolero* in the dynamic rhythms of Spanish folk dances.

## An age of unrest

The violent winds of change that were to create the nationalist impulse had their origins in the French Revolution of 1789 and the rise of Napoleon. The overwhelming triumph of the revolution in overthrowing the old order at it's outset showed that change was possible and the ancient regime was not necessarily as immovable as the hills. People all over Europe watched the progress of the Revolution in France closely.

Initially, the monarchs of Europe were not disturbed by thoughts that popular revolution could be dangerously contagious. But they were wrong, and the new 'philosophy' spread just as protestantism had done three centuries before. France extended an offer of French nationality to all peoples who aspired to be free—arguably another kind of empire building, but tempting nonetheless.

Even when the revolution finally collapsed, with Napoleon's defeat at Waterloo, it remained as an inspiration to intellectuals and radicals who believed they could overthrow the yoke of oppression in their own countries.

The old order was clearly worried and the Congress of Vienna in 1815 re-established the traditional, absolute monarchs wherever they could. The Habsburgs were restored to full power in Austria; Ferdinand VII returned to the throne in

*Louis Napoleon, nephew of the famous emperor, became president of the Second Republic in France established by the 1848 revolution. He was democratically elected, but within four years he had assumed absolute power and called himself Emperor Napoleon III, as this cartoon shows (above).*

Spain and proceeded to reverse all the changes made since 1808, the Bourbons returned in France; and in Italy sundry relations of the Habsburgs and the Bourbons became monarchs. Soon after, the Tsar of Russia initiated the Holy Alliance which pledged the signatories to maintain these arrangements by force if necessary.

But it was too late; the magic of kingship was already tarnished and the petty kings of Europe seemed to many to be mere puppets, as indeed many were, of powerful foreigners. Louis XVIII of France in particular could not even command the respect of his fellow aristocrats. Similarly, the Act of Holy Alliance seemed to many liberals to be a sinister and heavy-handed attempt to justify interference by despotic monarchs in the affairs of any small country in which liberal reforms were making progress. Soon there was a nationalist, revolutionary movement in nearly every country, from Ireland to Bohemia, striving to achieve its own role, independent of the great coalitions and family alliances of the past.

In nearly every country in Europe, governments relied on secret police and informers to keep these revolutionary movements under their thumbs. In Austria, Metternich set up his infamous 'system', which reached a peak with the terrible Carlsbad Decrees of 1819. In Russia, the Tsar deployed the notorious 'Third Section'. The revolutionaries were driven underground and began to form secret societies. But revolution continued to break out all over Europe between 1815 and 1848.

No country was entirely free of strife. In the 1820s, there were revolutions in Portugal, Spain, Greece, Poland, France, Belgium, Russia, Hungary and many other countries. The revolutions climaxed in the 'Year of Revolutions' – 1848 – when all the major powers of Europe felt the tremors of political upheaval.

On January 12 1848, the people of Palermo in Sicily rebelled against the misrule of Ferdinand II of Naples, and within weeks there were riots in nearly all the major Italian cities. At about the same time, a banquet celebrating a liberal victory at the polls in Paris was banned and the people of Paris instantly took to the streets in protest. These events sparked

*The victorious army of Giuseppe Garibaldi and his 'Red-shirts' enter Naples on 7th September 1860 (left). Garibaldi and his little army were the heroes of the struggle for Italian unification, playing a major part in the valiant defence of the short-lived Roman Republic of 1848, and conquering the kingdom of Naples in 1860.*

*Horrified by the terrible suffering caused by the economic depression of 1847, Karl Marx (top right) and his collaborator Friedrich Engels wrote the 'Communist Manifesto' to provide a strategy for social revolution. The document was to have far-reaching consequences and provide the rallying point for revolutionaries the world over. Giuseppe Mazzini (bottom right) typified the romantic nationalist movements of the early 19th century. Mazzini was a founder of the 'Young Italy' movement and a leading light in the 'Risorgimento'. It was Mazzini who led the short-lived Roman Republic of 1848.*

*Scenes like this (right) were commonplace particularly in eastern Europe as poor peasants, unable to pay their rent, were turned out in the cold.*

Novosti

Scala

off a chain of nationalist and popular insurrection all over Europe in Germany, Austria, Belgium, Switzerland, even in England. Yet despite the almost constant outbursts of revolution, the power base of the monarchs remained intact. The revolutions often seemed hopeless, heroic struggles against insurmountable odds. Few had any hope of succeeding, yet many hundreds of courageous men and women threw themselves into the fray. The revolutionary movements attracted many idealists and dreamers—romantics to the core.

Everywhere, the revolutionary movements of 1848 petered out. Indeed, few lasted beyond the end of the year. Sometimes, as in Prague, the retribution was bloody and terrible. The romantic belief in revolution suffered a severe setback. But it was clear that nationalism was an incredibly potent force in politics. Nearly all the revolutions of 1848 were essentially nationalist in character, and if the Hungarian, Czech and Polish movements were temporarily suppressed, the *Risorgimento* for the unification of Italy – then divided into numerous states under the influence of Austria-Hungary—and the nationalist movement in Germany were to change the face of Europe.

Revolutionaries in Europe became in many ways more realistic. The unification of Italy and Germany, finally achieved in 1871, was far from the heroic struggle of a few brave individuals that many would have liked. Germany's unification depended upon the cynical political manoeuvering of the Prussian chancellor Bismarck and the might and efficiency of the Prussian army, backed by developing Prussian industrial power. By defeating the Austrians and the French in battle, Prussia was able to unite Germany under the iron fist of the Kaiser and his Iron Chancellor Bismarck.

Similarly, the unification of Italy depended to a considerable extent on the political manoeuvering of Count Camillo di Cavour, the liberal leader of the Piedmont parliament. Perhaps with the best intentions, he engineered France into agreeing to help the Piedmont rid northern Italy of Austrian rule and combat the Papist forces of central Italy. Meanwhile, southern Italy was brought into the fold by

V. Vasnetsov 'Moving Day'/Novosti

*In the remote farming regions of eastern Europe, centuries-old traditions of costume, song and dance survived, providing artists with a rich heritage to draw upon. In Russia, in particular, always well outside the mainstream of European progress, the folk tradition still ran deep and women in elaborate traditional dress, like these women from the southern Ukraine, were a common sight.*

*The romantic image of the Bohemian rebel (right) provided the inspiration for many Czech composers such as Smetana and the whirling rhythms of Bohemian dances often infuse the music of the nationalists.*

a genuinely heroic effort by Garibaldi and his 'thousand' Red-shirts, who ousted the Bourbon king Francis II from Naples after a march from Sicily.

The smaller countries under the Austrian and Russian yoke had no such convenient allies to turn to. Instead, the revolutionary intellectuals looked to their own people for the impetus that would overthrow the status quo. Some intellectuals looked to the peasants and their national folk heritage. Others turned to the new working class, living and struggling to survive in the rapidly-expanding industrial cities. In the 1840s misery in these cities was rife as millions of people flocked to them only to find there was not yet enough work. Industrialists exploited the vast labour pool for cheap labour, and conditions for the working class were generally appalling. No wonder then that it was in 1848 that Karl Marx and Friedrich Engels formulated the now celebrated *Communist Manifesto* which declared that in the face of increasing misery the industrial proletariat would inevitably revolt and overthrow the property-owning bourgeoisie.

While southern and eastern Europe remained in the grip of terrible poverty and hardship, however, western Europe began to prosper, and by gradual social and political reform governments managed to dampen revolutionary fervour.

This then was the epoch epitomised by Offenbach's operettas (such as *La Vie Parisienne* and *Orpheus in the Underworld*), and it is an irony that this most frivolously French of composers was born in the German city of Cologne. Like Johann Strauss the Younger in Vienna, Offenbach created a deliberately light-hearted music, with a champagne sparkle. Perhaps he in Paris, like Strauss in Vienna, felt that the time of revolution, civil bitterness and conflict was — or should be — past, and sought to mirror a steadier and happier atmosphere in his splendidly light-hearted music. A little later, in Britain, W. S. Gilbert and Sir Arthur Sullivan were to perform much the

*Far away in the mists of the north, hidden by the massive shadow of the Russian empire, Finland was the forgotten country of Europe in the 19th century. But in the music of Jean Sibelius, so evocative of the trees, snow and mountains, and above all the hardy people of the icy North (right), Finland finally found its voice.*

same service for London with their Savoy Operas.

Yet neither Britain, France nor Austria were to escape the cataclysm that was eventually to engulf Europe in the early 20th century as the pressures for change provoked the great powers into the terrible events of 1914–1918.

Through the closing years of the 19th century and into the 20th, nationalism continued to fuel the fires of revolution. Insurgent nationalist forces in the myriad nations of Eastern Europe and the Balkans under the pall of Austrian and Turkish domination gave constant source of alarm to the old dynastic rulers of these vast territories. The power of the Habsburgs, worn down by a long succession of military defeats and rocked by a sequence of minor and major revolutions could not hold out against their demands forever. Sooner or later, these nations must break out on their own.

Moreover, the Russian Empire, keen to consolidate its power base, began to exploit the grand nationalist concept of 'Pan-Slavism' to encourage the Slavs in the Austrian Empire to revolt. Pan-Slavism was an ideal fostered by many Russian and Austrian Slav writers from the 1870s onwards, notably Feodor Dostoyevsky. Their belief was that after a long war between Russia and Europe, the Slavs would emerge victorious to found a united nation of all Slav peoples extending from the Baltic to the Adriatic to the Black Sea.

A similar concept, Pan-Germanism, began to grow in popularity amongst German people in northern Europe. Just as Pan-Slavists were often ardently anti-German, so Pan-Germanism tended to be anti-Slav and anti-Semitic. Both concepts were expansionist – and they wished to expand into the same areas. Some kind of clash was inevitable.

With so many nationalist undercurrents running through Europe, the great powers headed inexorably towards war. When Archduke Ferdinand of Austria was assassinated by an Austrian Serb in Sarajevo on 28 June 1914, it was simply the last straw, and nations were pitched into war with repercussions that even now still reverberate around the world.

*Mikhail Glinka (below) is regarded as the father of Russian nationalist music. In 1836, he wrote a startlingly successful opera called 'A Life for the Tsar' which was heavily influenced by the exotic rhythms of Russian folk music.*

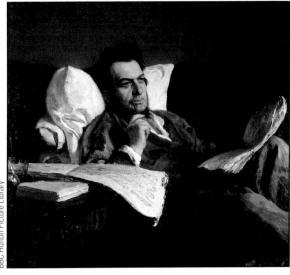

# LANDMARKS OF THE NATIONALIST ERA

### 1810–1830

**1815** Congress of Vienna ends Napoleonic Wars and re-establishes old European order. Forces of Nationalism ignored.
**1818** Great Powers meet at Congress of Aix la Chapelle to form Concert of Europe which promises mutual assistance against the forces of revolution.
**1821** Greek war of independence from Turkey.
**1822** British foreign minister Castlereagh dies.

Succeeded by George Canning who abandons Concert of Europe after Congress of Verona.
**1824** Louis XVIII of France dies. Charles X succeeds.
**1827** Battle of Navarino. Turkish fleet sunk by combined British, French and Russian fleet for failing to accept Great Power mediation in Greek war of independence.
**1828** Russia joins Greece in war with Turkey,

seeking to influence control of Straits between Med. and Black Sea.
**1829** Treaty of Adrianople gives Greece independence.
**1830** Belgium national revolt against Holland. Revolution in France establishes July Monarchy of Louis Philippe.

### 1831–1849

**1831** Hegel, mastermind of German thought stressing nationalism and total reverence to the state, dies.
Polish national revolt suppressed by Russia.
Giuseppe Mazzini founds 'Young Italy' which seeks to unite Italian Peninsula.
Belgium gains independence from Holland.
**1832** Great Reform Act extends franchise in Britain.
**1833** Treaty of Munchengratz—Prussia, Austria and Russia agree to cooperate in suppression of Polish

nationalism.
**1839** Mehemet Ali's wars against Turkey begin. Britain guarantees Belgian territorial integrity by Treaty of London.
**1841** Straits Convention. Turkey promises to close the Dardanelles during war.
**1842** Treaty of Nanking ends Sino-British Opium war.
**1845** Irish potato blight causes famine in Ireland.
**1847** Cavour forms 'Il Risorgimento' (The

Resurrection) to work for liberal, monarchical Italy. Californian gold rush.
**1848** Revolution throughout Europe in Sicily, France, Austria, Poland, Denmark, Germany, Italy, Britain, Ireland and Switzerland.
Louis Philippe falls. Metternich falls.
**1849** Reaction against revolutions. Russian troops intervene to defeat Hungarian revolt against Austria led by Kossuth.

### 1850–1870

**1854** Crimean war breaks out. Britain and France combine to stem Russian ambitions in the near East.
**1855** Nicholas II of Russia dies. Alexander II, a supporter of Pan-Slavism, succeeds.
**1856** Congress of Paris ends Crimean war.
**1858** Orsini bomb plot. Attempt on the life of Napoleon III reawakens his interest in Italian unity. Indian Mutiny against British rule.
Napoleon III meets Cavour and agrees Pact of Plombieres, promising French support to Piedmont in war against Austria.
**1859** War breaks out. Napoleon III so appalled by casualties at Battle of Solferino he sues for peace with Austria.

**1860** Garibaldi's march through Italian Peninsula. Italy unified.
Lincoln elected U.S. President.
**1861** Cavour dies, robbing new Italy of leader.
Alexander II emancipates Russian serfs.
Outbreak of U.S. Civil War.
**1862** Otto von Bismarck becomes Minister-President of Prussia.
**1863** Russo-Prussian agreement to quell nationalist uprising in Poland.
Confederates defeated at Gettysburg.
**1864** Prusso-Danish war over Schleswig-Holstein.
**1865** End of U.S. Civil War.
President Lincoln assassinated.

**1866** Austro-Prussian war. Austria defeated in seven weeks at Battle of Sadowa.
**1867** Ausgleich (Compromise) establishes Dual Monarchy of Austria-Hungary.
Slavonic Ethnographical Exhibition provides fillip to Pan-Slav movement.
Maximillian, Emperor of Mexico and brother of Franz-Josef of Austria-Hungary, executed.
Karl Marx publishes first volume of *Das Kapital*.
**1869** Suez Canal opened.
**1870** Franco-Prussian war. France defeated at Battle of Sedan. Napoleon III falls. Siege of Paris. New Empire proclaimed at Versailles.
Germany united.

### 1871–1890

**1871** Treaty of Frankfurt ends Franco-Prussian war. Alsace-Lorraine ceded to Germany.
Paris Commune.
**1872** Prusso-Russian-Austro Hungarian treaty signed; a union of Monarchies against revolution. France isolated.
**1874** Irish Home Rule party win over 50 seats at British general election.
**1875** 'War in Sight' Crisis between France and Germany.
Serbian revolt against Turkish rule; revolt in Hertzegovina.
**1876** Turkey commits Bulgarian atrocities.
Gladstone champions Irish cause in Britain.
**1877** Russia supports Pan-Slav movement and declares war on Turkey.
Sanjak of Novibazar, traditional centre of Serbian nationalism occupied by Austro-Hungarian troops to prevent union of Serbia and Montenegro.
**1878** Treaty of San Stefano ends Russo-Turkish war and establishes Bulgarian state.
Congress of Berlin revises San Stefano and returns Eastern Rumilia to Turkey. Confirms independence

of Serbia, Montenegro and Rumania.
**1879** Austro-German alliance against military aggression signed.
**1881** France occupies Tunis.
Alexander II of Russia assassinated by Polish student. Alexander III succeeds.
President Garfield assassinated.
1st Boer War.
**1882** Italy joins Austria-Hungary and Germany in Triple Alliance.
Britain annexes Egypt.
Phoenix Park murders harden English attitudes to Irish Home Rule.
**1883** Rumania joins 1882 Triple alliance.
**1884** Bismarck organizes Conference of Berlin to ease tension caused by imperialist rivalries of the Great Powers.
**1884-5** Germany joins scramble for Africa and annexes Tanganyika, Togoland and Cameroons.
**1885** General Gordon killed at Khartoum.
Nationalists in Indo-China defeat French army. Government of Jules Ferry falls.
**1886** Bulgarian crisis begins – Eastern Rumelia

unites with Bulgaria. Serbia demands compensation and is defeated by Bulgaria. Enlarged Bulgaria confirmed as autonomous principality.
**1887** Secret Reinsurance treaty signed between Germany and Russia, which de facto contradicts German promises to Austria-Hungary under terms of Dual Alliance.
**1888** Likelihood of war between Russia and Austria-Hungary mounts over Bulgarian crisis. Germany forces Russia to back down by publishing terms of Dual Alliance.
Kaiser Wilhelm I of Germany dies; Kaiser Frederick III succeeds, determined to liberalise Germany but dies after 90 days.
**1889** Crown Prince Rudolph of Austria-Hungary commits suicide at Mayerling.
**1890** Bismarck dismissed by Wilhelm II.
Luxembourg gains independence from Holland.

### 1891–1910

**1891** France and Russia move closer thereby ending French diplomatic isolation.
Construction of Trans Siberian railway begins.
**1893** Anglo-French imperialist aspirations clash over Siam.
**1894** Sino-Japanese war breaks out.
**1895** Japanese impose Treaty of Shimonoseki on defeated Chinese. Korea becomes independent.
Jameson Raid—abortive pro-British attempt to overthrow Boer Government of Paul Kruger.
Armenian massacres.
**1896** Kruger telegram—Anglo-German antipathy over Kaiser Wilhelm's congratulations to Kruger over defeat of Jameson Raid.
**1897** Germany seizes Kiauchow from China.
**1898** Russia annexes Port Arthur, and Britain Wei-hai-wei, from China.
Fashoda crisis. Diplomatic Anglo-French clash over the Sudan. French back down. Spanish-American war breaks out.

**1899** 2nd Boer War begins.
**1900** Boxer rebellion by Chinese nationalists against imperialism.
**1901** Australian Commonwealth proclaimed.
**1902** Arthur Griffin forms Sinn Fein (Ourselves Alone) to promote Irish independence.
Anglo-Japanese alliance signed.
Treaty of Vereeniging ends 2nd Boer war.
**1903** Suffragette movement founded in Britain.
**1904** Russo-Japanese war begins.
**1905** Bloody Sunday riots mark beginning of Russian revolution.
Kaiser Wilhelm's speech at Tangier sparks diplomatic crisis over Morocco.
Russia's Baltic fleet defeated by Japanese.
Russo-Japanese war ends.
**1906** Algeciras Conference on Morocco leaves Germany diplomatically isolated.
First military conversations between France and Britain in event of European war.

First Russian Duma (Parliament) held.
Finnish independence gained.
Anglo-Russian entente settles differences in Afghanistan, Persia and Tibet.
**1908** Young Turk revolution forces Sultan to grant a constitution.
Leopold II hands over Congo to Belgian Government.
Major diplomatic crisis caused by Austro-Hungarian annexation of Bosnia-Hertzegovina. Germany forces Russia to back down with threat of war.
**1909** British suffragettes stage hunger strikes.
General strike in Barcelona.
South Africa Act approves constitution of Union of South Africa.
**1910** Revolutions in Lisbon. Portuguese republic proclaimed.

### 1911–1914

**1911** Diplomatic crisis over Morocco occasioned by arrival of German gun boat 'Panther' at Agadir.
Italy declares war on Turkey. Invades Libya.
**1912** Chinese republic declared.
'Titanic' lost on maiden voyage with 1513 lives.
Italians occupy Rhodes.
Balkan states declare war on Turkey.
Italo-Turkish war ends. Libya ceded to Italy.
Woodrow Wilson wins US Presidency for Democrats.
**1913** Second Balkan war—Balkan league attacks Bulgaria.

Civil war threatened in Britain over Home Rule Bill. France extends military conscription to three years.
**1914** Irish Home Rule Bill passed by House of Commons, but does not receive Royal Assent because of outbreak of World War.
Franz Ferdinand, heir apparent to Austro-Hungarian throne, assassinated at Sarajevo by Gavrillo Princip.
Austria-Hungary declares war on Serbia, which escalates into general European war.
Panama Canal opened to traffic.
Russia defeated at Battle of Tannenberg.

German advance on Paris checked at Battle of Marne.
Germans attack Ypres.
Turkey declares war as ally of Germany.
Britain annexes Cyprus.
British naval victory at Falkland Islands.

# *The twentieth century*

*Never in the history of mankind has so much change, progress and development been made, in so many fields, as in the dynamic years of the 20th century.*

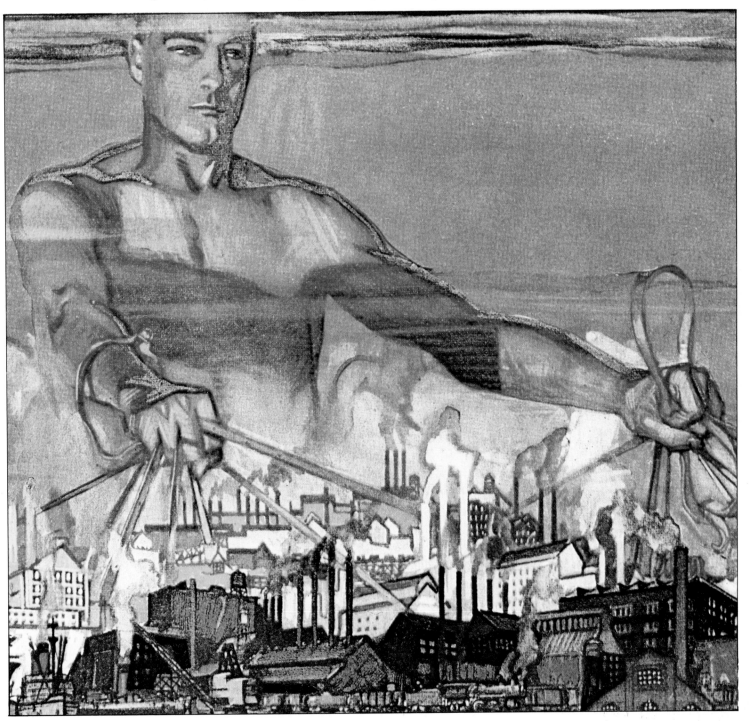

The 20th century has been a period of staggering, almost unbelievable change – a period of change perhaps more profound and far-reaching than any other in history. What man wrapped up against the cold on a horse-drawn omnibus in 1899 could have had any more than a vague notion of how his world was to be transformed in the next 100 years?

The idea that millions of people would be able to fly at high speeds in jet airplanes; that many diseases would be virtually eradicated from the world; that the monumental Russian, Chinese, Austrian, German and Turkish empires would vanish; that people would live in perpetual fear of weapons that could destroy the world many times over – all this would have seemed fanciful to him. Yet these are just a few of the startling changes that have already happened since 1900 – and the century is still not yet over.

Most significantly, perhaps, the 20th century has seen an incredible explosion of knowledge – scientific, technical, practical and social. The changes wrought by this new knowledge have altered life for those in the more privileged countries of the world as profoundly as any of the dramatic political events of the century.

### Scientific progress

Progress in every field of science has been breathtaking, none more so than physics. It was in 1905 that a young post office clerk in Switzerland named Albert Einstein published his theory on the 'relativity' of space and time that completely overturned traditional physics based on Newton's Laws of Motion. Relativity, along with the equally revolutionary 'quantum' theory that all energy is released in little bundles called 'quanta', provided the framework for a series of breakthroughs in atomic physics so far-reaching that even now Man is barely able to come to terms with them.

In the early years of the century, Rutherford demonstrated that the atom was like an ever-changing minute solar system, with electrons revolving round a nucleus like planets round the sun. By 1932 James Chadwick had discovered that the nucleus contained a tiny particle called the 'neutron'. Just seven years later, it was found that by bombarding a uranium atom with this particle, the atom could be split, thereby releasing the awesome power locked within it. By the end of World War 2, scientists had discovered how to use this power to make a terrifying bomb, a bomb that was used to completely destroy the Japanese cities of Hiroshima and Nagasaki, killing hundreds of thousands of men, women and children and leaving an awful legacy of suffering.

If progress in the other pure sciences has created nothing as awesome as nuclear weapons, it has affected our lives equally profoundly. The electron microscope has enabled biologists to explore the inner recesses of the basic unit of life, the living cell, and make some remarkable discoveries about the way life is both maintained and destroyed. The discovery, by Watson and Crick in 1953, of DNA, the molecule that provides a blueprint for life, unlocked the genetic code and opened the way for a series of

*The first half of the 20th century saw violence and destruction on a previously unimaginable scale in the form of two world wars. In World War 1 alone, over ten million people were killed and more than twenty million seriously injured – more than 20 times the casualties inflicted in any previous war. Even these figures actually disguise the terrible suffering of those who survived. Horrific scenes like this (right) permanently scarred the European consciousness.*

# LANDMARKS OF THE TWENTIETH CENTURY

|  | **1901–1910** | **1911–1920** | **1921–1930** |
|---|---|---|---|
| **Music** | **1901** Rachmaninov's *Piano Concerto no. 2;* Death of Verdi; Sibelius' *Symphony no. 2.* <br> **1902** Debussy's *Pelléas et Melisande.* <br> **1903** Sibelius', *Valse Triste.* <br> **1904** Puccini's opera *Madam Butterfly;* Death of Dvorak. <br> **1905** Debussy's *La Mer;* Lehar's operetta *Merry Widow;* Strauss's opera *Salome.* <br> **1907** Delius' opera *A Village Romeo & Juliette;* Death of Greig; Ravel's *Spanish Rhapsody;* Elgar's *Pomp and Circumstance.* <br> **1908** Mahler's *Song of the Earth;* Schoenberg's *Five Orchestral Pieces;* Death of Rimsky-Korsakov. <br> **1909** Mahler's *9th symphony.* <br> **1910** Stravinsky's *The Firebird;* Vaughan Williams' *Fantasia on a theme.* | **1911** Irving Berlin's *Alexander's Ragtime Band;* Death of Mahler. <br> **1912** Schoenberg's dissonant *Pierrot Lunaire* performed and attacked. <br> **1913** Stravinsky's *Rite of Spring.* <br> **1914** Vaughan Williams' *A London Symphony.* <br> **1915** Death of Skryabin. <br> **1916** Gustav Holst's suite *The Planets.* <br> **1917** Holst's *Hymn to Jesus.* <br> **1918** Prokofiev's *Classical Symphony;* Death of Debussy. <br> **1919** Bartok's ballet *The Miraculous Mandarin.* <br> **1920** Cocteau forms ragtime/jazz band 'Les Six'; Paul Whiteman's jazz band visits Europe. | **1921** Prokofiev's *The Love of Three Oranges.* <br> **1923** Arthur Honegger's *Pacific 231.* <br> **1924** George Gershwin's combination of classical music and jazz, *Rhapsody in Blue.* <br> **1925** Shostakovich's *First Symphony;* Berg's dissonant opera, *Wozzeck.* <br> **1926** First performance of Puccini's *Turandot.* <br> **1927** Stravinsky's *Oedipus Rex.* <br> **1928** Schoenberg's *Variations for Orchestra;* Ravel's *Bolero;* Gershwin's *An American in Paris.* <br> **1930** Stravinsky's *Symphony of Psalms.* |
| **History** | **1901** Queen Victoria dies. <br> **1902** Boer War ends. <br> **1904** Russo-Japanese war begins; Anglo-French entente. <br> **1905** Bloody Sunday riots in Russia; International crisis over Morocco. <br> **1906** Dreadnought launched. <br> **1907** Peace conference meets at The Hague. <br> **1909** Suffragettes stage hunger strikes. <br> **1910** Edward VII dies, George V succeeds. | **1911** International crisis over Morocco. <br> **1912** First Balkan war breaks out; Titanic sinks. <br> **1913** Civil War threatened in Ireland over Home Rule. <br> **1914** Outbreak of the First World War. <br> **1916** Battle of the Somme; Rasputin assassinated. <br> **1917** Bolsheviks seize power in Russia. <br> **1918** German surrender ends WW1; republic proclaimed in Berlin. <br> **1919** Treaty of Versailles signed between Germany and the Allies. | **1921** Irish Free State established. <br> **1922** Benito Mussolini establishes Fascist government in Italy. <br> **1924** Lenin dies; first Labour government elected in Britain. <br> **1925** Locarno Treaties establish Germany's western frontier and set up demilitarized Rhineland. <br> **1926** General strike in Britain. <br> **1929** Wall Street crash precipitates depression. |
| **The Arts** | **1901** Death of Toulouse-Lautrec; Picasso's first Paris exhibition. <br> **1903** Deaths of Paul Gauguin, Whistler and Pissarro; Bernard Shaw's *Man and Superman.* <br> **1904** Chekov's *The Cherry Orchard.* <br> **1907** Picasso's *Les Demoiselles d'Avignon.* First exhibition of Cubist paintings in Paris. <br> **1908** Epstein's sculptures *Figures.* <br> **1909** Diaghilev's first Ballets Russes season. <br> **1910** Post-Impressionists exhibition in London. | **1911** D. H. Lawrence's first novel *The White Peacock.* <br> **1913** D. W. Griffith's *Birth of a Nation;* D. H. Lawrence's *Sons and Lovers.* <br> **1914** Debut of Charlie Chaplin. <br> **1915** Buchan's *Thirty-Nine Steps.* <br> **1916** James Joyce's *Portrait of the Artist as a Young Man.* <br> **1918** Rupert Brooke's *Collected poems* published. <br> **1919** Gropius founds Bauhaus School. | **1921** Picasso's *Three Musicians;* rise to stardom of Rudolph Valentino; BBC formed. <br> **1922** James Joyce's experimental novel *Ulysses.* <br> **1924** E. M. Forster's novel *A Passage to India;* deaths of Franz Kafka and Joseph Conrad. <br> **1925** Gropius's Bauhaus buildings, Dresden; Scott Fitzgerald's *The Great Gatsby.* <br> **1927** First talking movie, Al Jolson in *The Jazz Singer.* <br> **1928** D. H. Lawrence's *Lady Chatterley's Lover;* Walt Disney's *Steamboat Willie* starring Micky Mouse. |
| **Science and Technology** | **1901** Marconi demonstrates wireless. <br> **1902** The Curies isolate pure salt uranium. <br> **1903** Wright brothers make first flight. <br> **1904** Ivan Pavlov wins Nobel Prize for his work on the conditioned reflex. <br> **1905** Albert Einstein proposes theory of relativity. <br> **1909** Louis Blériot flies the English Channel. | **1911** Rutherford predicts, with Nils Bohr, the structure of the atom. <br> **1914** Argote shows citrate prevents clotting of blood, thereby making transfusion possible. <br> **1915** Junkers company construct first metal aeroplane. <br> **1916** Einstein proposes general theory of relativity. <br> **1917** de Sitter proposes relativistic model of the expanding Universe. <br> **1919** Rutherford splits the nucleus of an atom. | **1921** Marie Stopes establishes first birth control clinic in London. <br> **1922** Sigmund Freud's *The Ego and the Id,* proposes structure of human personality. <br> **1923** Hubble demonstrates existence of other galaxies. <br> **1924** Introduction of tuberculosis vaccine. <br> **1925** Introduction of open heart surgery by Souttar. <br> **1926** John Logie Baird invents television. <br> **1928** Alexander Fleming discovers penicillin. <br> **1930** Whittle patents first practical jet engine. |

Imperial War Museum

## 1931–1940

**1931** Ravel's *Piano Concerto in G Major;* Bartok's *Piano Concerto no. 2.*
**1934** Deaths of Delius, Holst and Elgar.
**1935** Gershwin's *Porgy and Bess* – folk opera.
**1936** Prokofiev's *Peter and the Wolf.*
**1937** Deaths of Gershwin & Ravel.
**1938** Bartok's Violin Concerto.

## 1941–1950

**1941** Benjamin Britten's *Sinfonia da Requiem.*
**1943** Death of Rachmaninov.
**1944** Copland's ballet *Appalachian Spring.*
**1945** Britten's opera *Peter Grimes;* Bartok dies in poverty.
**1946** Menotti's opera *The Medium.*
**1949** Death of Richard Strauss.

## 1951–1965

**1951** Stravinsky's opera *The Rake's Progress.*
**1953** Death of Prokofiev.
**1954** Milhaud's *La Riviere Endormie.*
**1955** Death of Arthur Honegger.
**1956** Cole Porter's *High Society* songs; Presley's rock 'n' roll albums.
**1957** Stravinsky's ballet *Agon;* Death of Sibelius.
**1958** Death of Vaughan Williams and Buddy Hofly.
**1962** The Beatles release *Love Me Do;* Britten's *War Requiem.*

---

**1931** Spanish monarchy overthrown; Japan occupies Manchuria.
**1932** Nazis gain 250 seats in German Reichstag elections.
**1933** Hitler appointed German Chancellor.
**1934** Hitler becomes Führer of Germany.
**1936** George V dies; Spanish Civil War begins.
**1937** Spanish village of Guernica destroyed by German air raid.
**1938** Munich Crisis over German annexation of Czechoslovakian Sudetenland; Anschluss of Germany and Austria.
**1939** General outbreak of Second World War.

**1941** Japanese attack on Pearl Harbour; Siege of Leningrad.
**1943** Mussolini falls; Tehran Conference of Allied Powers.
**1944** 'D-Day' landings. Assassination attempt on Hitler.
**1945** Yalta Conference of Allied Powers; Roosevelt dies; Mussolini executed; final defeat of Germany & suicide of Hitler; Atomic bombs dropped on Japan.
**1947** Indian and Pakistani independence; Marshall aid to Europe.
**1948** Assassination of Gandhi; Israel established.
**1949** NATO formed; Chinese Communist Republic established.
**1950** Korean war begins.

**1951** First USSR atom bomb.
**1953** Stalin dies; end of Korean war.
**1956** Soviet troops crush Hungarian revolt.
**1957** Treaty of Rome establishes EEC.
**1958** De Gaulle comes to power in France.
**1960** J. F. Kennedy elected to US Presidency.
**1961** East Germany erects Berlin Wall.
**1962** Crisis over Khrushchev's supply of missiles to Cuba.
**1963** Kennedy assassinated.
**1964** Nehru dies; Khrushchev resigns.

---

**1931** Death of ballerina Pavlova.
**1932** Aldous Huxley's *Brave New World.*
**1935** T. S. Eliot's *Murder in the Cathedral.*
**1936** First BBC television broadcast; deaths of Chesterton, Gorky and Kipling.
**1937** Disney's *Snow White;* Picasso's *Guernica.*
**1938** Orson Welles's broadcast of *War of the Worlds.*
**1939** David O. Selsnick's *Gone with the Wind;* Steinbeck's *The Grapes of Wrath.*
**1940** Graham Greene's *The Power and the Glory.*

**1941** Orson Welles's film *Citizen Kane.*
**1942** Walter de la Mare *Collected Poems.*
**1943** Rogers & Hammerstein musical *Oklahoma.*
**1944** Moore's sculpture *Madonna and Child.*
**1945** Orwell's *Animal Farm;* Waugh's *Brideshead Revisited.*
**1946** Jean-Paul Satre's *Existentialism and Humanism.*
**1947** Tennessee Williams play *A Streetcar Named Desire.*
**1948** Graham Greene's *The Heart of the Matter.*
**1949** George Orwell's last novel *Nineteen Eighty-Four.*
**1950** Le Corbusier's Ronchamp chapel; Death of Bernard Shaw.

**1951** Alfred Hitchcock's film *Strangers on a Train.*
**1952** First performance of Agatha Christie's *The Mousetrap.*
**1953** Kingsley Amis's *Lucky Jim;* Samuel Beckett's *Waiting for Godot.*
**1954** J. R. R. Tolkien's *Lord of the Rings* trilogy.
**1956** Utzon completes design of Sydney Opera House; Osborne's *Look Back in Anger.*
**1958** Frank Lloyd Wright designs Guggenheim Museum.
**1960** Fellini's *La Dolce Vita.*
**1963** Moore's *Three Reclining Figures.*

---

**1931** Electron microscope developed by Ruska.
**1932** James Chadwick discovers the neutron.
**1934** Focke develops first practical helicopter.
**1935** Radar developed by Watson-Watt.
**1936** First manufacture of polythene.
**1937** Strassmann and Hahn observe nuclear fission of uranium; first radio telescope.
**1939** Magnetic tape recording demonstrated; Death of Freud.
**1940** Frisch and Peierls' memo on possiblity of atom bomb.

**1941** Whittle's jet engine successfully tested on an aeroplane.
**1942** German V1 rockets go into production.
**1944** First workable mechanical computer.
**1945** First electronic computer designed.
**1947** First supersonic air flight; Introduction of radioactive carbon dating.
**1948** Invention of transistor; publication of Kinsey's *Sexual Behaviour in the Human Male.*
**1949** First high altitude photograph of the Earth obtained.

**1951** Fermi proposes theory of origin of cosmic rays.
**1952** Morgan charts spiral structure of Milky Way; Contraceptive pill inroduced.
**1956** First kidney transplant.
**1957** USSR launches first satellite 'Sputnik 1'.
**1958** Lunik III gives Russians first photograph of dark side of the moon; British hovercraft crosses Channel.
**1960** Yuri Gagarin becomes first man to orbit the earth.
**1962** John Glenn becomes first US astronaut; US explodes nuclear bomb in outer space.

experiments in genetic manipulation – experiments with enormous implications only now starting to be appreciated.

These advances in the pure sciences have been paralleled by technological progress. Engineering has helped man to realize his dream of flying; and to provide him with skyscrapers, jet propulsion and the internal combustion engine, on a massive scale. In the field of medicine the century has so far seen such landmarks as the discovery of antibiotics and effective vaccines which have all but eradicated some of the worst killer diseases from the world. Scanners using radiation and ultrasonics have made diagnosis of illnesses much easier and major organ transplant is now commonplace.

Psychology has also made rapid progress in the 20th century, although it is true to say that the work of Freud and Watson did not provide such a comprehensive bedrock as, say, Einstein's or Darwin's contribution to their respective fields of science. Psychology has shifted away from the notion of mind and mental conflicts towards a complete study of the individual interacting with the environment. The effect has been to widen understanding of human behaviour and experience, and to alleviate some of the stresses which are the new product of the 20th century world.

### The artistic revolution

Man has been blown along like tumbleweed in a hurricane by the progress of science. Not surprisingly, Europe's new technological image was reflected in the arts of the first 30 years of the period. Painters, writers, poets and composers, sensitive to the rapidly changing society around them and to the deepening spiritual and moral dilemmas created by such profound changes, showed in their respective work all the symptoms of a culture in rapid transition. After World War I, there was wholesale abandonment of traditional concepts of taste, technique and form in the arts. Experiments with

Mary Evans Picture Library

*The early years of the century saw startling developments in every facet of society. In science, Albert Einstein (above) demonstrated the 'relativity' of space and time and revolutionized man's understanding of physics. In the field of transport technology Louis Blériot flew the English Channel to end Britain's splendid isolation. But for women, the work of Marie Stopes (below) in championing the use of contraceptives had a much more profound effect.*

Sir Gerald Kelly/The National Portrait Gallery

free verse, abstract painting and music lacking conventional harmonies and melodies reflected the search for a new form of expression to suit the new disharmonious world.

Some artists sought to escape this discord between man and the environment through introspection. The popularization of psychology led them to explore the inner consciousness as the only reliable indicator of what experience meant.

Many more mirrored the modern image of the times in their work. The 'modernist' revolt in the arts immediately after World War I reflected this mood, and painting led the way for the other arts to follow. The Surrealist movement rejected representational painting, preferring instead incongruous imagery, while the Cubists, inspired by primitive art, experimented with abstract designs of deliberate distortion and destruction.

In music as well, traditionalism and orthodoxy were superseded as new styles illustrated the lack of harmony and even alienation between composers and their new social environment. The last flickerings of the great Romantic flame, kept burning by the music of Richard Strauss and a few others, finally guttered out in the wind of change. Traditional forms, harmonies and melodies were gradually overthrown by a wave of experimentation, re-appraisal and theorizing. Music became notably more intellectually-based and, like art, less immediately approachable to the general public. Composers like Stravinsky and Prokofiev shocked the world with their dynamic, propulsive pieces that seemed to revel in dissonance and harmonies that grated on ears used only to the traditional sounds of western music. Composers like Schoenberg baffled the public with music based on an entirely new tonal system called 'serial' music, which used all the twelve notes of a series rather than eight.

Interestingly, the shock of the new technology drove many composers to experiment with primitive rhythms and tonalities. In a way, it was an expression of the violence and disintegration that they saw in modern society. In another, it was a

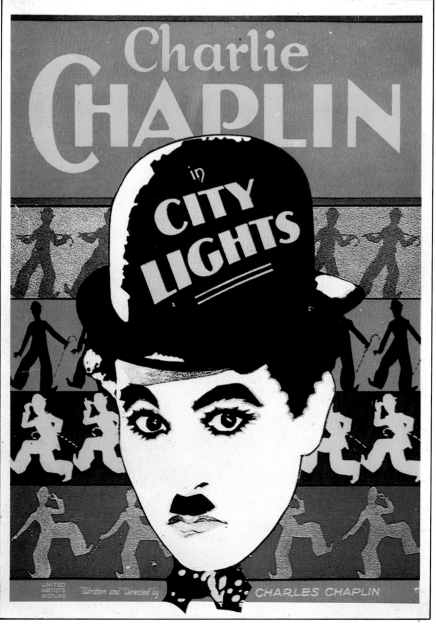

*In the years between the wars, industry and art began at last to cater for the masses. Mass-production techniques (above right) made the Model 'T' Ford the first million-selling car. And Hollywood turned out hundreds of popular films that made stars like Charlie Chaplin (right) universal heroes.*

search for a raw power in their music that they could not find by any other means, a replacement of individual romantic emotion by primitive, universal passion. For some composers, the inspiration was the wave of African and Asian music that began to be heard for the first time. For composers like Bartok and Rodrigo the rhythms and sounds of their native folk music became the driving force.

It was folk music, too, which proved to be a key element in the remarkable revival of English music in the early years of the century, when Elgar, Holst and Vaughan Williams wrote some of this country's most dearly-loved music. But the new music and art forms did not remain in vogue for long. By the late 1920s the spread of education had created a new mass civilization demanding mass culture.

## Mass communication

For many, the convulsively distorted imagery of new art forms, the experiments with distorted music, and the apparent destruction of the English language by literary figures like Joyce were seen as pretentious and incomprehensible. Instead, mass society preferred the Charleston, ragtime and jazz. Chaplin, Pickford, Gershwin and Honegger became the idols of the 1920s, as the growth of the film industry, escapist writing and popular music reflected the demands of mass society.

Glittering cinemas sprung up all over Europe, especially in Britain. In Liverpool, it was estimated that 40 per cent of the population went to the cinema once a week, and 25 per cent went twice. The movies revolutionized the pattern of life. Women could join their husbands in their leisure as they never could in the public house or at the

*A chance observation of mould led to the discovery by Alexander Fleming (above) in 1928 of penicillin, the first of the antibiotics that enabled doctors to cure a wide range of diseases.*

*In the 1920s, jazz (above right) became the first of a long series of popular music styles, aimed exclusively at the young, that stretches right down to the electro-pop of today.*

*The inter-war years also saw the rise of fascism in many European countries, though nowhere did it take hold quite as terrifyingly as in Germany. In the cartoon (right) Hitler is satirized in the days before he came to power trying to sell 'Mein Kampf' to old father Germany.*

football ground. During the depression of the 1930s, it has been said, the cinema averted revolution!

The spread of radio and also the invention of the telephone and television made the 20th century the age of mass communication, which has effectively 'shrunk' the world. The later part of the period has seen the increasing use of mass communication in political affairs. In the 1930s, Goebbels used the radio with great effectiveness to generate popular support for Hitler, while F. D. Roosevelt used it to extend his Presidency into almost every home in the United States. Successful use of television debates won John Kennedy the 1960 presidential election against Richard Nixon, and in many countries in the 1970s and 1980s, serious political debate has often been replaced by television selling of presidential-style national leaders. Television has brought pictures into our homes from across the world, and is responsible for the development of culture and the

shaping of artistic and economic tastes. It is against this backcloth of a society rapidly developing in all directions that the great political events of the century have unfolded.

### The collapse of Empires

In 1900, Europe was the centre of the world. European imperialism and exploration had extended to all four corners of the globe, imposing European style and culture wherever it went. Of the great superpowers of today, the United States was a slumbering giant, determined to keep out of the affairs of the old world; and semi-feudal Russia teetered on the brink of revolution as the most backward of the European powers. In 1900, the Habsburg, Hohenzollern and Romanov royal families dominated the continent. Now, a few countries retain a monarchical system, but no royal family in Europe has any real power.

When the 20th century opened it seemed no power could withstand the might of European arms and commerce. Today only the vestiges of European power remain. Between 1945 and 1960, no fewer than 40 countries and a quarter of the world's population revolted against colonialism and won their independence. Never before in the whole of history has so revolutionary a change taken place so rapidly. The American black leader, William Du Bois, made this remarkably astute prophesy in 1900: 'The problem of the 20th century is the problem of the colour line – the relation of the darker to the lighter races of men in Asia and Africa, in America and the islands of the sea.' At one and the same time, the 20th century has seen the impact of the developed world on Africa and Asia, and the revolt of Africa and Asia against their rulers. This impact can be attributed largely to western industry, technology and science. Having transformed European society, it had the same cataclysmic effect throughout the other continents where European culture spread. Colonialism also often led to the creation of a western-educated elite in many countries where European ideas were spread, and these people frequently took the lead in organizing indigenous resentment against the Europeans into powerful nationalist movements.

### The 'German problem'

Before World War I all the governments of Europe faced irresistible social and political forces at home, notably the rise of either Nationalism or Socialism or both. Germany, in particular, responded to these forces by adopting an erratic and vacillating foreign policy which served to unite Britain, France and Russia against her. This in turn intensified Germany's fear that she was being encircled by a ring of hostile powers. Germany's attempt to break out of this encirclement came at a time when all the major European powers were willing to go to war, since they saw in war the means of diverting and diffusing domestic tensions which were the product of the new century.

For Russia, the war did not, in the long run, serve this purpose. The Bolshevik revolution of 1917, brought about by the excesses of war and Tsardom, presented a general threat to the established order in Europe.

American involvement in World War I in 1917 tipped the balance decisively in favour of the Allied powers, but at the end of the conflict America abdicated the responsibility foisted upon her by virtue of her growing economic might. While the Soviet Union withdrew into a world of famine, terror and Stalinist purges, the USA declined the leadership of the world. Europe, though poorly equipped, was left to fend for herself, through the economic collapse of the 1930s and the consequent rise of Hitler, Mussolini and Franco.

The German problem remained to manifest itself in unspeakable cruelty on a scale never before witnessed in human history. World War II was

*The 20th century has seen the people of the world's two largest nations, China and Russia, free themselves of imperial rule and adopt a communist system. In Russia, it was Vladimir Ulyanov (Lenin) who was the hero of the revolution; in China, it was Chairman Mao Tse Tung whose thoughts guided the people (above left).*

*Increasing population and urbanization forced man to build upwards as well as outwards and, for many people, nothing seems to symbolize the fast-living urban lifestyle of the 20th century better than the myriad lights and towering skyscrapers of Manhattan at night (left).*

20 miljoen kinderen verhongeren

HELP

UNAC giro 9600

especially brutal on the Eastern front, where Russians and Germans almost drowned in each other's blood: an experience which has done much to shape Russian fears and foreign policy to this day. The eventual defeat of Hitler left an immense power vacuum in the centre of Europe into which the two superpowers were drawn. In the end, America resorted to using the new-found power of atomic bombs to bring victory over Japan, Hitler's allies in the Pacific. 'This is the greatest thing in history,' said an excited President Harry Truman, when news of the Hiroshima bomb was reported to him.

The war left Europe decimated, no longer able to control its own destiny without the say so of the superpowers. America and the Soviet Union stared at each other in adversity and mutual paranoia across a devastated Europe. The long period of cold war throughout the austere 1950s gave way, after the Korean war, the invasion of Hungary and the Berlin blockade, to a new era in East-West relations. Detente grew, even though the 1962 Cuba crisis nearly led to a nuclear exchange.

Whereas the future of European history in 1900 seemed bright and assured, today it is uncertain. The methods of fascist dictatorships, and the experiences of two world wars have badly dented European vitality. Beyond the ever present threat of nuclear destruction lie the chronic problems of an expanding world population, pollution of the environment, exhaustion of our raw materials and serious economic problems, notably unemployment. But the history of the 20th century has been a period of notable achievement as well as misery. We must retain the hope and belief that 100 years from now these problems will have been curtailed, and that the 20th century will represent the beginning of a new era, rather than the end of one.

*In the 20th century, Man saw the world from the outside, in space, for the first time (below), but often failed to see the hardship within created by the uneven technological and material progress that made this possible. Appeals to help the hungry in the 'Third World' are a striking feature of European life in the late 20th century (left).*

# Modern musical instruments

*A musical instrument is any object or device (excluding the human voice) that can be used to produce musical sounds. By this definition, a plate struck rhythmically with a spoon is a musical instrument and, though a composer may not have called for this particular effect, some have required odd instruments: Mahler asked for a blow from a hammer in his Sixth Symphony and Schoenberg for clanking chains in the Gurrelieder; and less seriously, the British humorist, Gerard Hoffnung, commissioned a piece scored for four vacuum cleaners! However, although modern inventions like the electronic synthesizer have been used in serious music – such as Honneger's oratorio, Joan of Arc at the Stake – most composers still rely on the instruments of the modern symphony orchestra and on a few other modern instruments that are not, strictly speaking, members of the orchestra.*

MODERN MUSICAL INSTRUMENTS

# The symphony orchestra

*The symphony orchestra is so much a fixture of the modern musical scene that it is surprising to discover that it is a comparatively recent development. Until the mid-1500s, music was merely the accompaniment to human voices (the word, orchestra, derives from the Greek for the space in front of the stage where the dance or orchesis was performed by the chorus). By the early Baroque period (c.1600), composers were writing purely instrumental music played by an orchestra comprising strings and a few woodwind instruments. The orchestra as we know it took shape in the Classical period, with the division into the four 'families' – strings, woodwinds, brass and percussion. Some composers, notably Berlioz and Mahler, have required huge orchestras, but most modern composers score for the conventional orchestra, sometimes adding instruments like the piano, guitar or saxophone.*

# The symphony orchestra

*The standard disposition of the modern symphony orchestra is illustrated below. Of course, the arrangement will vary from orchestra to orchestra, depending on factors such as the piece being played, the setting, the purpose of the performance and the preferences of the conductor. In addition, a particular symphony may require more or fewer instruments. The key on the right shows the grouping of the instruments by category and name.*

1: 1st violins, 2: 2nd violins, 3: Violas, 4: Cellos,
5: Double basses, 6: Piccolo, 7: Flutes, 8: Oboes,
9: Cor anglais, 10: Clarinets, 11: Bass clarinets,
12: Bassoons, 13: Double bassoon, 14: Harps,
15: Horns, 16: Trumpets, 17: Percussion,
18: Timpani, 19: Trombones, 20: Tubas.

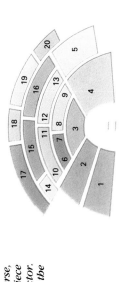

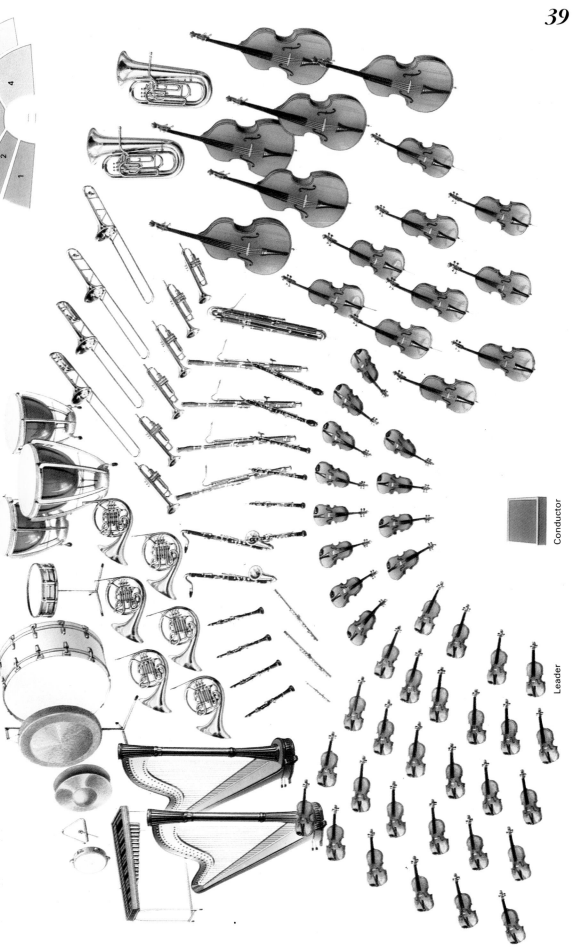

Conductor

Leader

Brian Delf

MODERN MUSICAL INSTRUMENTS

# *Stringed instruments*

*In the modern symphony orchestra, the family of stringed instruments consists of the violin, viola, cello and double bass. These instruments are generally considered to be the 'first family' of the orchestra, and their 'head' (the first-violin player) is the leader or concert master of the orchestra. Stringed instruments hold this place not only in Western music, but also in early music and in the music of other civilizations. This is because the stretched strings can be rapidly and accurately tuned, and produce clear notes of fundamental pitch. This results in instruments of great range and power of expression, and all the great Western composers from the Baroque period to the 20th century have exploited the family's versatility.*

# The violin

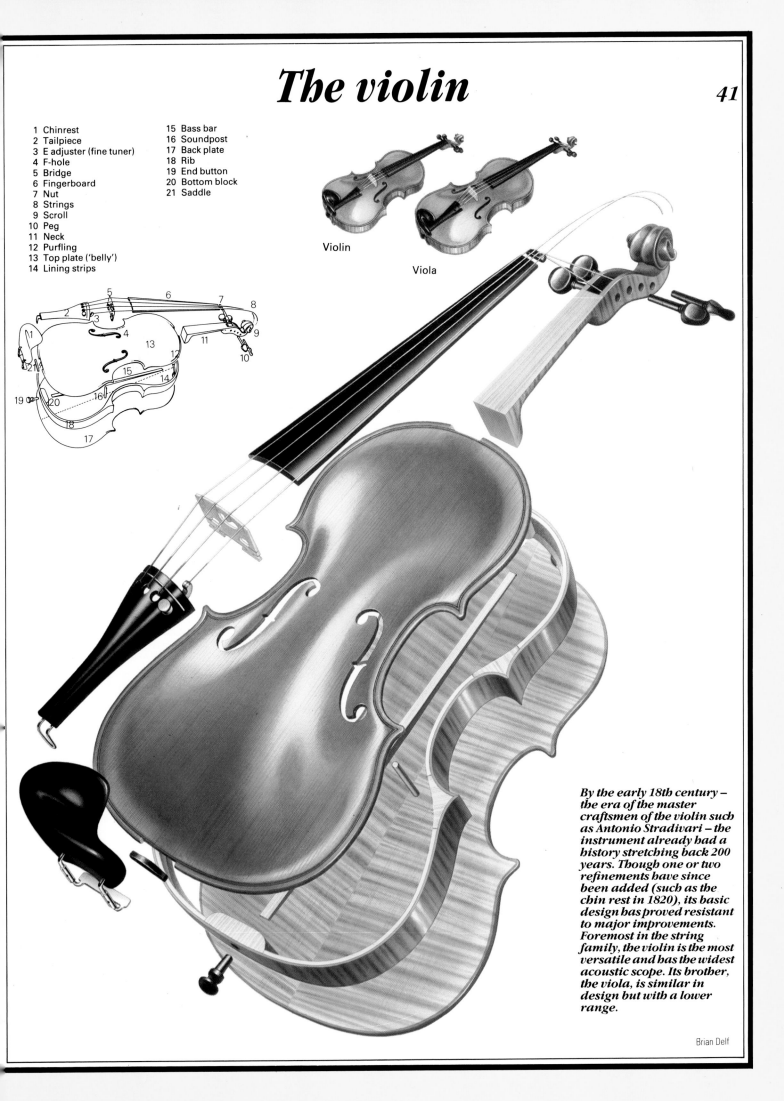

1 Chinrest
2 Tailpiece
3 E adjuster (fine tuner)
4 F-hole
5 Bridge
6 Fingerboard
7 Nut
8 Strings
9 Scroll
10 Peg
11 Neck
12 Purfling
13 Top plate ('belly')
14 Lining strips
15 Bass bar
16 Soundpost
17 Back plate
18 Rib
19 End button
20 Bottom block
21 Saddle

Violin

Viola

By the early 18th century – the era of the master craftsmen of the violin such as Antonio Stradivari – the instrument already had a history stretching back 200 years. Though one or two refinements have since been added (such as the chin rest in 1820), its basic design has proved resistant to major improvements. Foremost in the string family, the violin is the most versatile and has the widest acoustic scope. Its brother, the viola, is similar in design but with a lower range.

Brian Delf

# The cello

Properly known as the 'violoncello' the cello originated in the early 16th century, but it was some time before its present size and appearance were eventually arrived at. Played upright, it was once gripped between the calves. A tail spike was introduced in the 18th century, allowing the player to rest the instrument on the floor, but it was not until the end of the 19th century that the adjustable tail spike was used. This small innovation immediately allowed the cellist greater freedom of position and movement.

Double Bass      Cello      Viola   Violin

Brian Delf

# *The double bass*

Early double bass

Three views of the modern double bass

Dating from the early 16th century the double bass has had a chequered history, going through various five- and six-string phases before arriving at its present four strings. And for convenience of playing it has lost its violin-like shape (top left) and gained more steeply sloped shoulders. The 'f holes', too, have varied over the years. Not until the middle of the 18th century did the orchestra regularly include the double bass. Now the symphony orchestra usually employs eight of them where their combined effect lends both force and a basic rhythmic structure. In jazz bands the instrument is played pizzicato: the strings are plucked with the fingers rather than bowed, as in a symphony orchestra.

Over 200 concertos have been written for the double bass and its champion composers have included Mozart, Schubert, Strauss, Mahler and Britten.

Brian Delf

# Woodwind instruments

*The woodwind family consists of the flute and piccolo, the oboe, the cor anglais or English horn, the clarinet and bass clarinet, the bassoon and double bassoon and, when it is added to the orchestra, the saxophone (page 70). Woodwind instruments are not necessarily made of wood, though they often are; for example, the modern flute is usually made of metal (though some players still prefer the wooden flutes that were manufactured until the 1940s). All members of the family – apart from the flute and piccolo – are fitted with a flexible reed or reeds through which the player blows air. As air passes over the reed, it vibrates to form the sound. On the flute and piccolo, the solid, fixed mouthpiece across which the player blows air, acts as the reed. The player then presses keys or covers fingerholes in the instrument to produce the notes required by the score.*

# The flute and the piccolo

*The flute dates back to the Old Testament and the Ancient Egyptians. The term 'flute', however, covers a wide range of instruments – many bearing little resemblance to the modern flute (below). The modern design is based on a shape devised by Theobold Boehm in 1847; in trying to achieve a greater range of sound the holes were enlarged so much that a mechanical means had to be found to cover them. Boehm achieved this by using a system of rods and pads.*

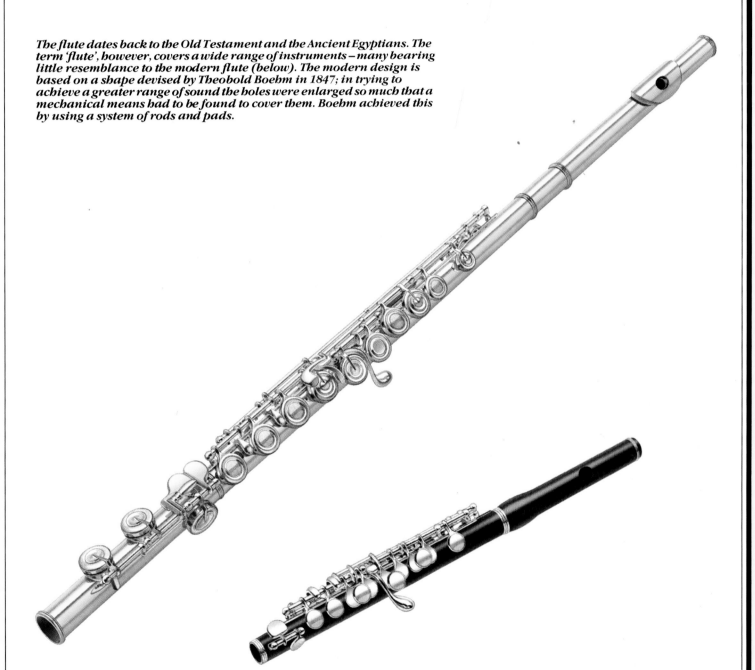

*The piccolo (above) is half the size of the flute and is pitched an octave higher. The Boehm mechanical keys were added much later than to the flute. As with the flute the sound is made by the player blowing across the opening, causing the column of air within the instrument to vibrate. The piccolo achieved prominence in the late 18th century and, although it was Beethoven who first included it in major orchestral works – the Fifth and Sixth Symphonies – Tchaikovsky was the composer who provided it with its most splendid orchestral passages.*

Brian Delf

# *The oboe*

*Illustrated below is the modern oboe – separated into its reed plus its three main sections, and assembled. This soprano woodwind instrument, which is made from ebonite, plastic or metal, has 16 to 20 side holes. Of these, six are directly under the player's fingers and the remainder are controlled by intricate mechanisms – a refinement added in the 19th century. The double-reed principle of the oboe, though acoustically very complex and quite difficult for the player to master, is one that can be traced back to ancient history. The characteristic 'reedy' sound has been described as being perhaps the most tender and expressive in all wind music.*

# The cor anglais

*The cor anglais, otherwise known as the English horn, first made its appearance towards the end of the 17th century. It is the tenor member of the oboe family, and is pitched a fifth lower than the oboe. Its shape varied greatly in its early years – from completely straight, gently curved, to sharply angled. The origins of its distinctive bulb-shaped bell (which it shares with the other larger oboes, the oboe d'amore and the bass oboe) are unknown, and recent research has shown that it does not have a great effect on the instrument's tone. The cor anglais moderne was made by Brod in 1839, and used a curved crook to hold the reed, in order to overcome the instrument's ungainly length and provide a comfortable playing position. Since then it has undergone major improvements.*

*With a rich, deep sound, the cor anglais is generally used for long, slow, plaintive solos, such as in the slow movement of Dvořák's New World Symphony or Sibelius's The Swan of Tuonela. Most professional oboists will possess a cor anglais, though they will not often be asked to play it.*

Brian Delf

# The clarinet and bass clarinet

Usually made of wood, the clarinet has a cylindrical bore and a single reed mouthpiece. The instrument was first developed from the chalumeau by the German Johann Denner in about 1700, and radically improved in the late 1800s with the adoption of the Boehmn system of keys and fingering, previously devised for the flute. There are several varieties in use, the most common being the soprano, pitched in B flat. Perhaps the best known pieces for clarinet are Mozart's Quintet and Concerto, but Weber, working with virtuoso players, did much to explore its potential.

The bass clarinet is also pitched in B flat, an octave below the soprano. Developed in the mid 1800s by the Belgian instrument maker Adolphe Sax, inventor of the saxophone, it was used regularly by Mahler and Wagner towards the end of the 19th century.

Brian Delf

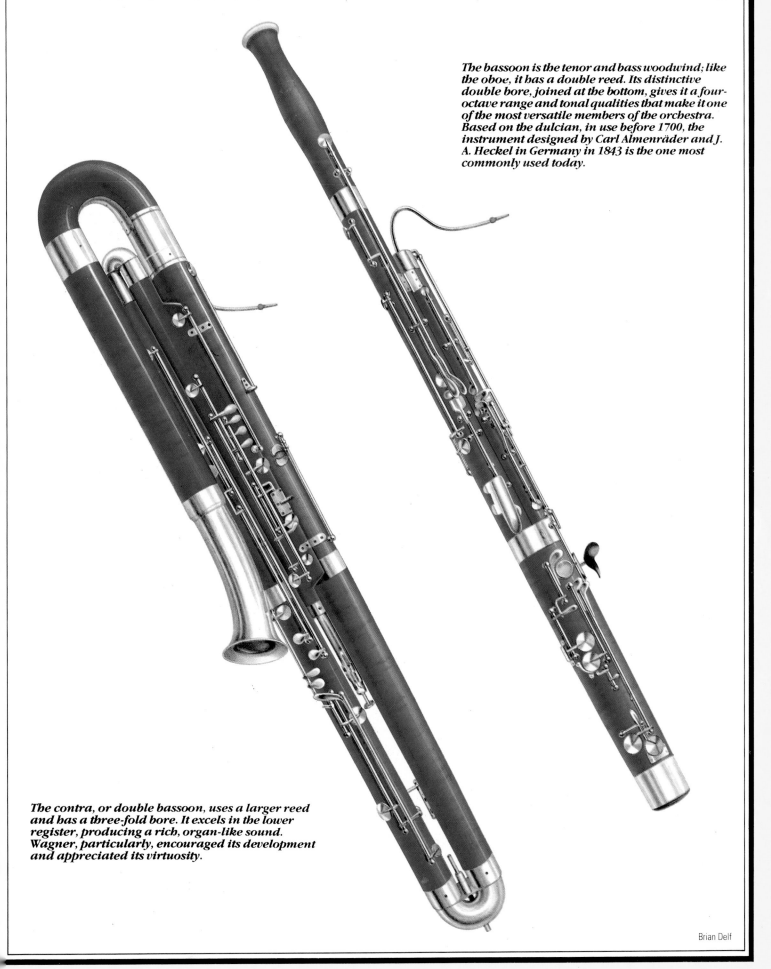

*The bassoon is the tenor and bass woodwind; like the oboe, it has a double reed. Its distinctive double bore, joined at the bottom, gives it a four-octave range and tonal qualities that make it one of the most versatile members of the orchestra. Based on the dulcian, in use before 1700, the instrument designed by Carl Almenräder and J. A. Heckel in Germany in 1843 is the one most commonly used today.*

*The contra, or double bassoon, uses a larger reed and has a three-fold bore. It excels in the lower register, producing a rich, organ-like sound. Wagner, particularly, encouraged its development and appreciated its virtuosity.*

Brian Delf

**MODERN MUSICAL INSTRUMENTS**

# *Brass instruments*

*Brass instruments, like the woodwind family, are wind instruments, the sound being produced by the player's air or 'wind'. In the brass family, the player's lips act like the woodwinds' reed, in that, when they are placed against a cup- or vase-shaped metal opening in the instrument they vibrate as the air passes through them. The exact sound produced depends on the length and width of the instrument's tubing, the player's use of its valves or (in the trombone) slide, and the shape of its belled opening. In the symphony orchestra, the brass family consists of the trumpet, trombone, French horn and the tuba. Occasionally, however, other members of this large family, which are usually used in jazz and marching or military band music – such as the cornet or euphonium – may be included if they are required for the performance of a particular work.*

Brian Delf

# The trumpet

In ancient times the trumpet, used as a military and ceremonial instrument, was a long, straight tube with a flared bell at one end. By the 17th century, this 'natural' trumpet had acquired the much more portable, bent shape it still basically has, and was used extensively by Bach and other Baroque composers. The valves were added in the early 19th century by German makers, greatly improving the instrument's range. The three-valve B flat model is most often used in the orchestra today, although a wide range of higher and lower keyed versions has been developed. Berlioz, in the 1830s, was one of the first to write for the valve trumpet and Mahler, Strauss and Stravinsky went on to compose interesting orchestral parts for it. But only in jazz has it been fully exploited as a solo instrument, most of the current technique being pioneered by Louis Armstrong in the 1920s and 30s.

Brian Delf

# The trombone

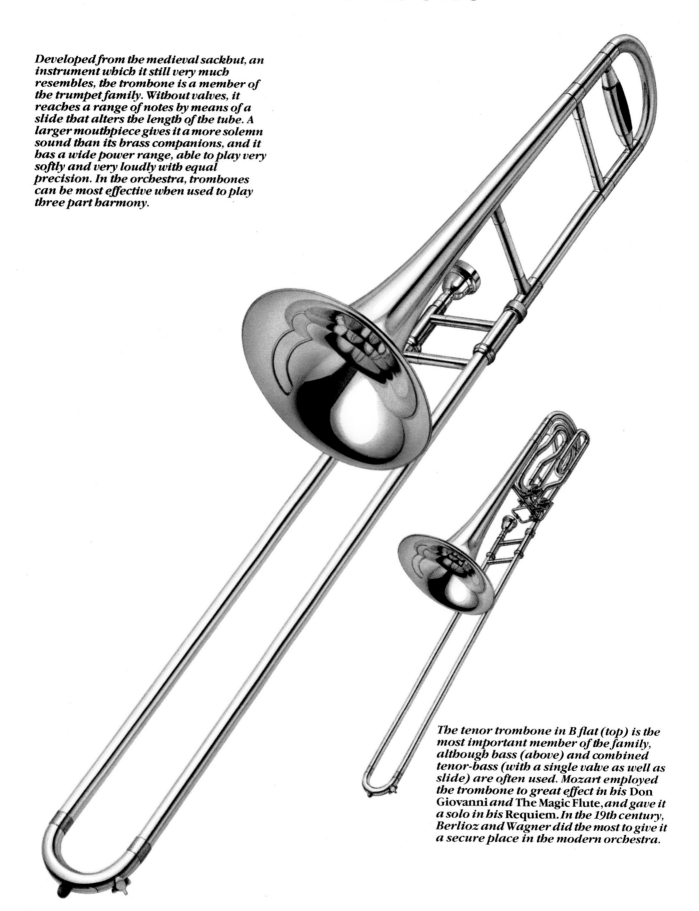

Developed from the medieval sackbut, an instrument which it still very much resembles, the trombone is a member of the trumpet family. Without valves, it reaches a range of notes by means of a slide that alters the length of the tube. A larger mouthpiece gives it a more solemn sound than its brass companions, and it has a wide power range, able to play very softly and very loudly with equal precision. In the orchestra, trombones can be most effective when used to play three part harmony.

The tenor trombone in B flat (top) is the most important member of the family, although bass (above) and combined tenor-bass (with a single valve as well as slide) are often used. Mozart employed the trombone to great effect in his Don Giovanni and The Magic Flute, and gave it a solo in his Requiem. In the 19th century, Berlioz and Wagner did the most to give it a secure place in the modern orchestra.

Brian Delf

# *The French horn*

The European orchestral, or French, horn is based on early
hunting horns first used orchestrally in the early 18th
century. Valves, usually three, were added about a century
later. Design was revolutionized around 1900 with the
development of the B flat/F double horn, now the most
common in use. Having a softer, more mellow tone than other
brass instruments, horns are often used to sustain
harmonies, and act as auxiliaries to the clarinets and
bassoons.

In 1849, Schumann became one of the first to compose for
the valve horn. Tchaikovsky later gave it an important
'romantic' passage in his 5th Symphony, and Richard Strauss
showed its power as a solo instrument.

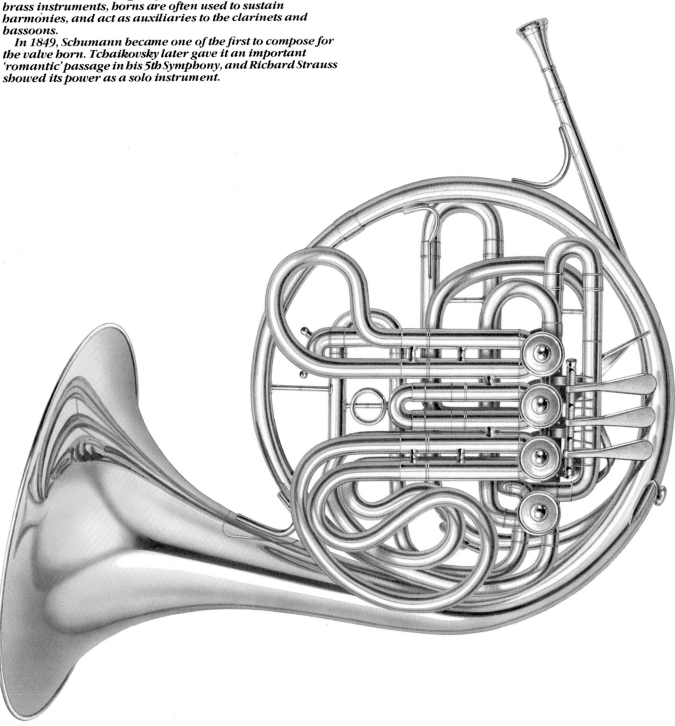

Brian Delf

# The tuba

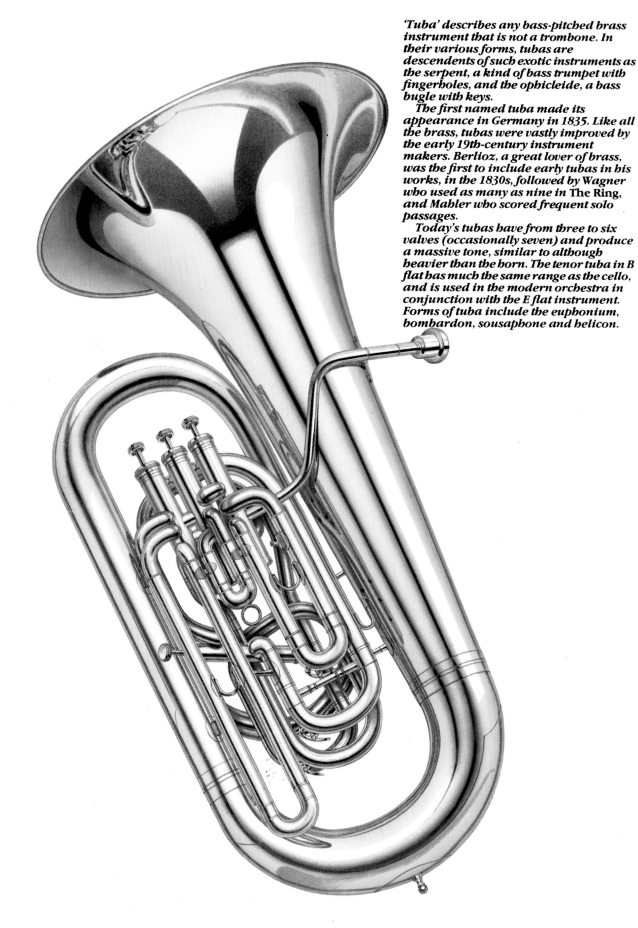

'Tuba' describes any bass-pitched brass instrument that is not a trombone. In their various forms, tubas are descendents of such exotic instruments as the serpent, a kind of bass trumpet with fingerholes, and the ophicleide, a bass bugle with keys.

The first named tuba made its appearance in Germany in 1835. Like all the brass, tubas were vastly improved by the early 19th-century instrument makers. Berlioz, a great lover of brass, was the first to include early tubas in his works, in the 1830s, followed by Wagner who used as many as nine in The Ring, and Mahler who scored frequent solo passages.

Today's tubas have from three to six valves (occasionally seven) and produce a massive tone, similar to although heavier than the horn. The tenor tuba in B flat has much the same range as the cello, and is used in the modern orchestra in conjunction with the E flat instrument. Forms of tuba include the euphonium, bombardon, sousaphone and helicon.

Brian Delf

**MODERN MUSICAL INSTRUMENTS**

# *Percussion instruments*

*Percussion instruments are those which produce a sound when shaken or struck, and because of this the family contains some of the most varied and some of the oldest instruments known to humanity. The family can be sub-divided into drums (timpani, tambourine, bongos), wood (castanets, maracas, xylophone), and metal (gong, triangle and bells). Most percussion instruments cannot produce sounds of definite pitch – the glockenspiel, timpani, xylophone and tubular bells are among the exceptions – and so their use is, in the main, confined to adding rhythm or colour to the orchestral sound. The percussion section in the modern symphony orchestra consists of the various drums, the cymbals and tambourine, the xylophone and glockenspiel, and the gong, bells and triangle. However, the possible size of this family is almost infinite and may include objects not usually thought of as musical instruments if the composer requires them.*

# The tambourine and the cymbals

*One of the oldest members of the percussion section, the tambourine is often used to add a touch of exotic colour, usually Spanish or Oriental. The drum head (tambour is the French for drum) can be struck in a variety of ways by the hand and fingertips or on the bent knee. A moistened thumb slid steadily along the rim of the head produces a continuous trill. For an extensively long trill, two players may be needed, the second to continue when the first runs out of rim. In Petrushka, Stravinsky calls for it to be dropped to the floor to represent the limp body of the puppet falling dead.*

*The rather simple shape of the cymbals belies a highly complicated manufacturing process tinged with a hint of mystery. Some of the best orchestral cymbals are made today with the addition of a secret alloy first formulated in the early 17th century in Istanbul. After casting, the cymbals are flattened by rollers, shaped to form the cup and trimmed and hammered into shape with precision instruments. Each side is then carefully grooved and the instruments are left to age. Cymbals of various sizes are used in the orchestra. To clash, they must be passed over each other at a correct angle, otherwise an embarrassing air lock may stick the two together. They can also be used to make a less spectacular contribution to the orchestral sound by sliding the faces over each other. Dvořák specified a precise vibrating period for the cymbals when he used them in his symphony* From the New World, *while in Tchaikovsky's* Romeo and Juliet *overture, they serve rather aptly to illustrate the clash of swords in the duel scene.*

Brian Delf

# The drums

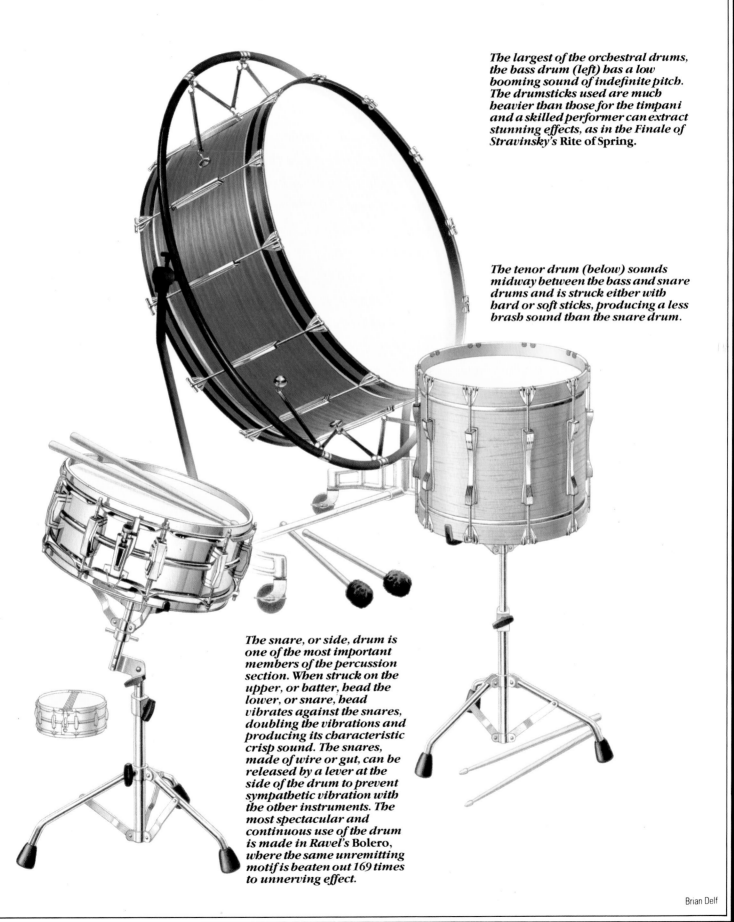

The largest of the orchestral drums, the bass drum (left) has a low booming sound of indefinite pitch. The drumsticks used are much heavier than those for the timpani and a skilled performer can extract stunning effects, as in the Finale of Stravinsky's Rite of Spring.

The tenor drum (below) sounds midway between the bass and snare drums and is struck either with hard or soft sticks, producing a less brash sound than the snare drum.

The snare, or side, drum is one of the most important members of the percussion section. When struck on the upper, or batter, head the lower, or snare, head vibrates against the snares, doubling the vibrations and producing its characteristic crisp sound. The snares, made of wire or gut, can be released by a lever at the side of the drum to prevent sympathetic vibration with the other instruments. The most spectacular and continuous use of the drum is made in Ravel's Bolero, where the same unremitting motif is beaten out 169 times to unnerving effect.

Brian Delf

# The timpani

Brian Delf

The timpani, or kettle drums, are the only drums which participate in the harmony of the orchestra as they can be tuned to a definite pitch. Like the other drums, their origins are military and they were inspired by those originally encountered in the crusades which were played mounted on horse or camel. Each drum consists of a resonating bowl of copper and a head of stretched calfskin or plastic. The drum's size and the tautness of the head determine the range of pitch; and though Berlioz, with characteristic extravagance, has scored for 16, an orchestra normally uses three to five of varying sizes, to prevent too wide a range of tuning for each drum. Timpani are tuned manually by screws or by foot pedals which may be connected to a tuning gauge which indicates the pitch (above). Varying playing techniques produce different results. Handel employed them to thrilling effect in the 'Hallelujah' chorus and Haydn, himself a timpanist, used them to open his 'Drumroll' symphony, as did Beethoven for his Violin Concerto, while Tchaikovsky in the Finale of Romeo and Juliet used them to simulate heartbeat. Twentieth-century composers have written increasingly demanding parts for the timpani, including concertos and solo works.

# The xylophone and the glockenspiel

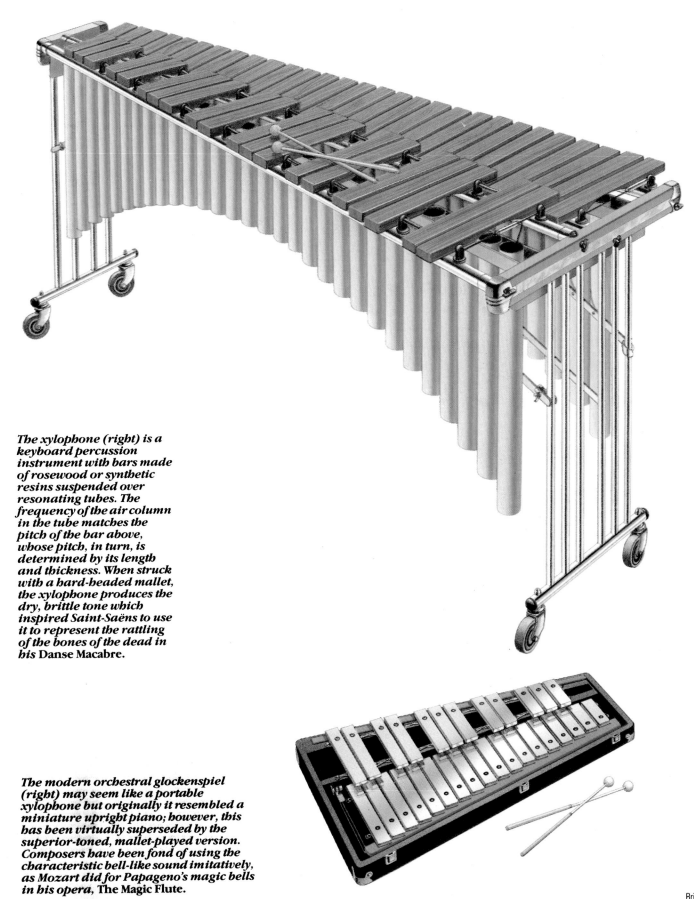

The xylophone (right) is a keyboard percussion instrument with bars made of rosewood or synthetic resins suspended over resonating tubes. The frequency of the air column in the tube matches the pitch of the bar above, whose pitch, in turn, is determined by its length and thickness. When struck with a hard-headed mallet, the xylophone produces the dry, brittle tone which inspired Saint-Saëns to use it to represent the rattling of the bones of the dead in his Danse Macabre.

The modern orchestral glockenspiel (right) may seem like a portable xylophone but originally it resembled a miniature upright piano; however, this has been virtually superseded by the superior-toned, mallet-played version. Composers have been fond of using the characteristic bell-like sound imitatively, as Mozart did for Papageno's magic bells in his opera, The Magic Flute.

Brian Delf

# The gong, the bells and the triangle

Of distinctly oriental pedigree, the gong (right) provides the characteristic 'splash' of sound. Composers often do not distinguish between it and the tam-tam which has no definite pitch but is very similar in appearance. The orchestral gong is about three feet in diameter and, depending on the vibrations of the beating spot, can produce a volume of sound of amazing resonance. Tchaikovsky used it to great effect in his Pathétique symphony.

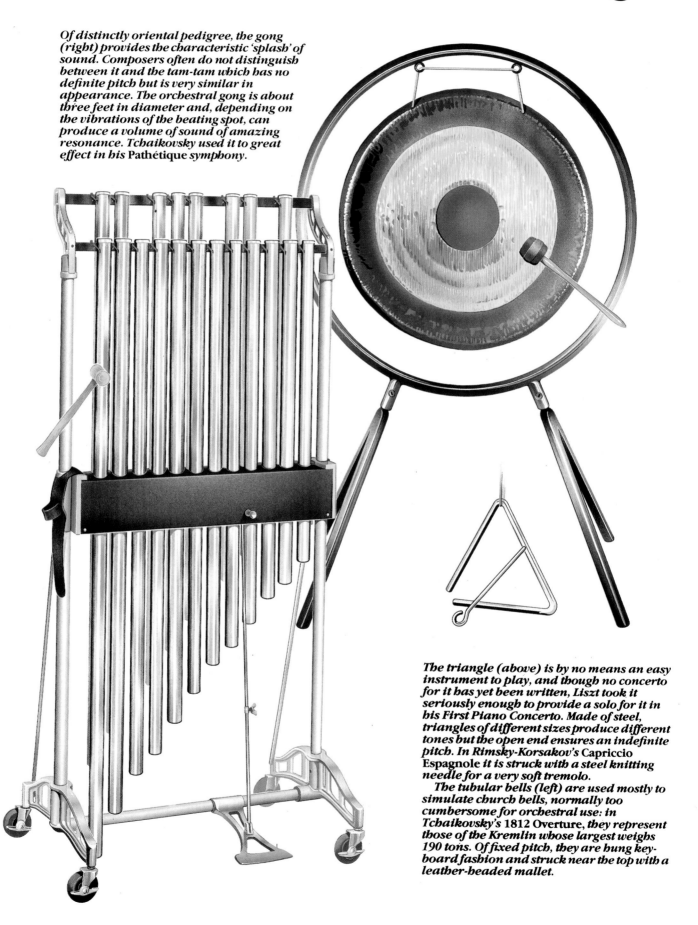

The triangle (above) is by no means an easy instrument to play, and though no concerto for it has yet been written, Liszt took it seriously enough to provide a solo for it in his First Piano Concerto. Made of steel, triangles of different sizes produce different tones but the open end ensures an indefinite pitch. In Rimsky-Korsakov's Capriccio Espagnole it is struck with a steel knitting needle for a very soft tremolo.

The tubular bells (left) are used mostly to simulate church bells, normally too cumbersome for orchestral use: in Tchaikovsky's 1812 Overture, they represent those of the Kremlin whose largest weighs 190 tons. Of fixed pitch, they are hung keyboard fashion and struck near the top with a leather-headed mallet.

Tony Lodge

# *Other modern instruments*

*The following pages describe nine modern instruments that either feature in classical music performances as solo instruments – the most obvious example being the piano – or are used to add colour or novelty to the orchestral sound. Of these instruments, only the harp is a formal member of the orchestra, though others, like the lute and harpsichord, have an equally distinguished musical history. Some of these nine instruments, in contrast, were invented comparatively recently – in the case of the saxophone in the middle of the 19th century. There are, of course, many other modern musical instruments (most usually heard in jazz and rock music) that occasionally perform with the orchestra, but this is at present rare. However, the orchestral family may grow, especially as modern composers seek to exploit the capabilities of instruments like the electronic synthesizer.*

# *The harp*

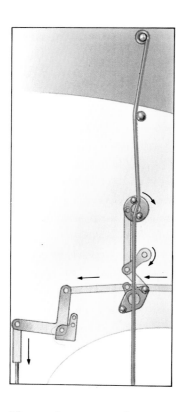

*The modern concert harp (right) is a result of several innovations. The 46-47 strings are tuned to the scale of B, with the C strings coloured red, and the Fs, blue. Thanks to the double action (above) patented by Sébastien Erard in 1810, the pitch of each string can be raised twice by a semitone. By depressing one of the seven pedals through a notch, a rod in the pillar activates a series of intricate and delicate levers. These levers turn discs through which the strings are wound, thus shortening the length of the string for that note of the scale. The repertoire has kept pace with the technical improvements: Mozart's Concerto for Flute and Harp was written for a much lighter instrument, while Wagner wrote extremely demanding passages. The rippling tones were much appreciated by the Impressionists, especially Ravel and Debussy.*

Brian Delf

# The guitar

The guitar, though not part of an orchestra, is one of the most popular musical instruments today. The modern classical guitar owes its present shape and size to the model created by the Spanish maker, Antonio de Torres, in the second half of the 19th century. It has six strings fixed at the lower end over a bridge and tightened at the head by pegs which in turn operate rollers, over which the strings are wound. The underside of the face, or table, is reinforced with struts which greatly improve the quality of the sound. The guitar has been a favourite of many composers: Schubert sang his songs to it as did Weber. Berlioz took it seriously but criticized the facile compositions of non-playing composers. And Paganini abandoned the violin for three years in favour of the guitar. However, the Spaniard, Fernando Sor, and the Italian, Mauro Giuliani – both accomplished guitarists – did much to establish the instrument with a more serious repertoire of solo works and concertos in the last century. But it was the tireless zeal of Andrés Segovia that gave the classical guitar its respectable status as a concert instrument today, and inspired a new generation of highly-accomplished artists. The most popular works still remain in the Spanish idiom, such as Rodrigo's Concierto de Aranjuez and Fantasia para un Gentilhombre.

Tony Lodge

# The lute and the mandolin

*Though no music has been written for it for nearly two centuries now, the lute has the largest repertoire of any instrument, apart from the piano. Several wooden ribs are shaped, bent and glued together individually to form the body while the intricate rose is carved out directly from the soundboard. The very fine gut strings are tuned in pairs, and to prevent the extremely fine soundboard from bending under the tension of the strings, it is supported internally by a series of bars glued to the back which also contribute to the lute's clear, silvery tone. The heyday of the lute was the 16th and 17th centuries, and though Bach wrote four solo suites, almost all the music was composed by lutenists themselves, among whom the Elizabethan, John Dowland, gained unique international fame.*

*The mandolin, with its several regional variants, was originally indigenous to Italy; but the one we know now is the Neapolitan, whose belly bends down at its widest part. Though similar in appearance to the lute, its artistic contribution is much less impressive. Its eight wire strings are plucked with a plectrum, either with a stroking technique or with the more characteristic repeated sounding or tremolando, which helps sustain its rather insubstantial sound. The soundhole is not quite round and a plate below it protects the wood against the plectrum. Most of its music was written in the 18th century when the mandolin was also incorporated into the orchestra of operas, where it makes its most famous appearance (on stage) in the serenade in Mozart's Don Giovanni.*

Brian Delf

# The harpsichord

*Until it was finally superseded by the piano in the mid-18th century, the harpsichord had been the supreme keyboard instrument since the beginning of the 16th century, especially during the Baroque era. There are usually three series, or choirs, of strings and as many jacks as there are choirs, resting on the inner end of each key which plucks the strings. Many harpsichords have two manuals (keyboards): the lower one for sounding all the strings of a note and the upper one, for sounding one string. Stops which protrude from above the manuals operate various mechanisms that affect the tone. Long after its eclipse by the piano, the harpsichord continued to be used in opera as continuo. In spite of its limitations (unknown, of course, at the time), the harpsichord's plangent tones were exploited to the full by Baroque composers, notably François Couperin and Domenico Scarlatti – the greatest of harpsichordists.*

Brian Delf

# *The grand piano*

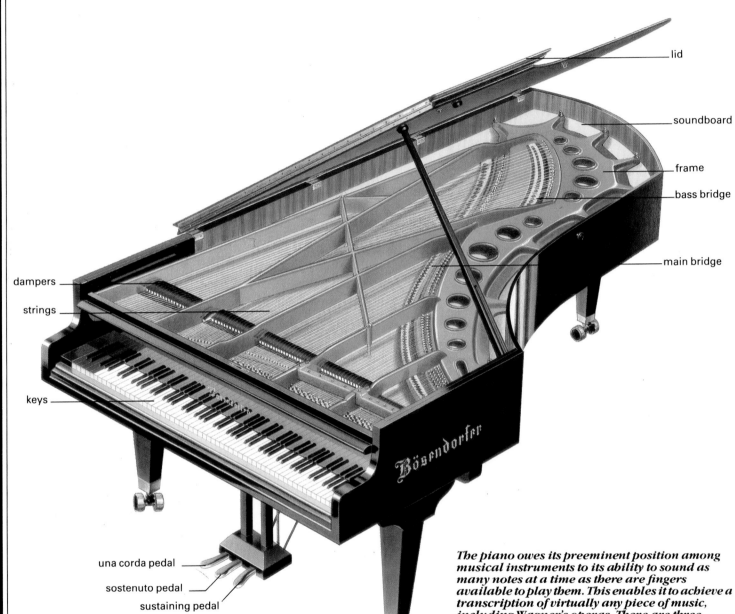

lid

soundboard

frame

bass bridge

main bridge

dampers

strings

keys

una corda pedal

sostenuto pedal

sustaining pedal

The piano owes its preeminent position among musical instruments to its ability to sound as many notes at a time as there are fingers available to play them. This enables it to achieve a transcription of virtually any piece of music, including Wagner's operas. There are three strings per treble note, two per tenor and one per bass. When they are struck by the felt-headed hammers, the bridges on the massive iron or steel frame convey the soundwaves to the soundboard which makes them audible. An intricate mechanism ensures that the hammer falls back as soon as it has struck, while a damper descends on the strings as soon as the key is released. The right, or sustaining, pedal keeps all the dampers raised while it is depressed, allowing notes to sound after the keys are released, while the middle, or sostenuto pedal only raises the damper for the note which it is depressed for. The left, or una corda pedal moves all the hammers sideways so that they strike only two strings per note and produce a more muted sound. The piano's repertoire is the largest and most varied, encompassing early keyboard pieces like C. P. E. Bach's elegant sonatas and the 20th-century composer Kaikhosru Sorabji's virtually unplayable and unplayed Opus Clavicembalisticum, which lasts nearly three hours.

## The action

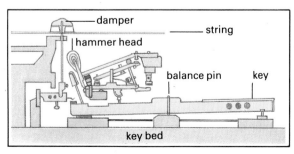

damper

string

hammer head

balance pin

key

key bed

Brian Delf

# *The upright piano*

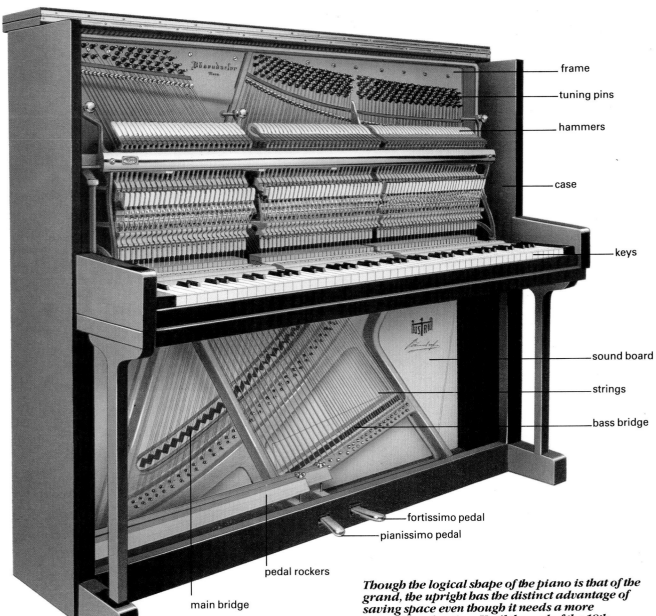

- frame
- tuning pins
- hammers
- case
- keys
- sound board
- strings
- bass bridge
- fortissimo pedal
- pianissimo pedal
- pedal rockers
- main bridge

## The action

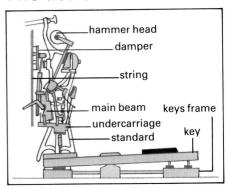

- hammer head
- damper
- string
- main beam
- undercarriage
- standard
- keys frame
- key

*Though the logical shape of the piano is that of the grand, the upright has the distinct advantage of saving space even though it needs a more complicated action. Until the end of the 18th century, the upright was basically a grand set vertically – some early models were nicknamed 'Giraffe'. However, by the early 19th century, less ungainly versions of the upright were invented independently in Philadelphia and in Vienna. The smaller, 'cottage' piano became such a popular feature of middle-class households that it was even built in with beds or tables. By World War I, piano manufacture had changed drastically, resulting in mass-assembled factory uprights at nearly half the price of a handcrafted grand. The piano immediately became accessible to a much greater market and enjoyed its heyday as a major source of home entertainment before the advent of the gramophone or broadcasting. The presence of a piano in every parlour also meant a plethora of easily-playable, pleasing pieces such as* Warblings at Dawn *and* Warblings at Eve *and, of course, the much-maligned* Maiden's Prayer. *The piano was also incorporated into jazz where it continues to enjoy a significant position.*

Brian Delf

# *The player piano*

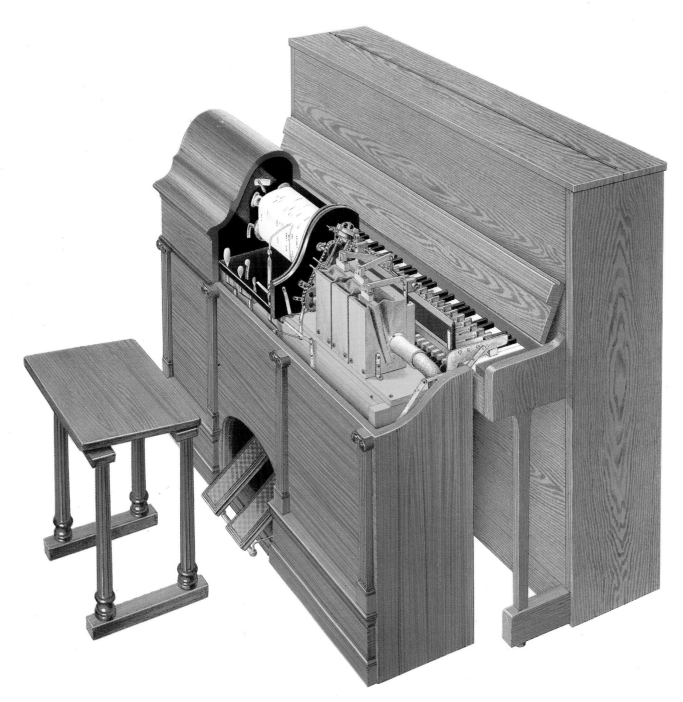

At the height of the piano's popularity, there were still many people whose desire to possess one far exceeded their ability to play. In 1920, 70 per cent of the pianos manufactured in the USA were player pianos. These were either the 'pianola' type (above) – where a separate playing device was connected to an ordinary piano, or the reproducing type where the playing mechanism was incorporated within the piano.

Both types work on the same basic principle, in which an intricately and accurately punched roll of paper unrolls over a tracker bar which has holes in it corresponding to the keyboard. When the two sets of holes coincide, suction created by the pedals is conveyed through a network of tubes and valves which operate the wooden 'fingers'. Volume and speed can be controlled by the speed of pedalling and by hand-operated levers, allowing the player unlimited creative control over the performance. Even though coin-operated models were sited in cafés, the repertoire and appeal of the player piano was not entirely frivolous. It was taken seriously enough by leading composers to produce music for it, such as Stravinsky's Etude pour Pianola. The U.S. composer Conlon Nancarrow also composed music specifically for the player piano.

Brian Delf

# The organ

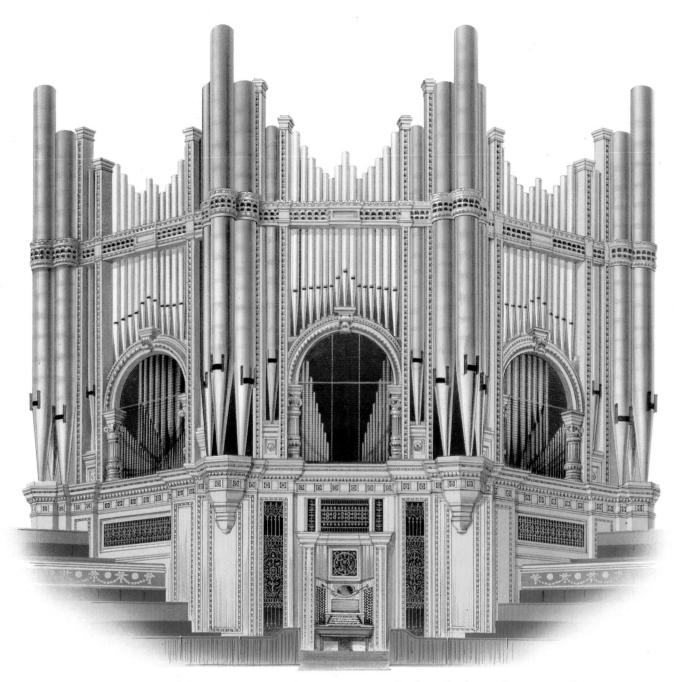

Mozart called the organ 'the king of musical instruments' – a fitting title for what is one of the largest and most complex of instruments. The earliest known organ (from Alexandria) dates from the 3rd century BC, and all subsequent models have been composed of the same basic elements, with variations to permit different 'colours' or tonal effects. The sound an organ produces is made by air resonating in the pipes, and involves air being blown mechanically through ranks of pipes via one or more keyboards or manuals. The means of supplying the air have varied with developments of the instrument's design and have included: hydraulic pressure, in very early designs; huge bellows operated by the blowers' body weight – as many as 70 organ blowers have been used on larger instruments; electrical, rotary fans; and player-operated bellows on the portative or portable organ.

Each rank of pipes has its own characteristic tone, which usually imitates that of a wind instrument, but can also mimic the sound of the string and percussion families. Each rank has a slider which covers the mouths of the pipes and allows them to sound when the players open a stop or knob on the console. The combination of several ranks, manuals and stops, and also a pedal board, as found on large cathedral or concert hall organs, such as the one in the Albert Hall, London (above), can produce a formidable array of sound from the thunderous to the angelic. Throughout its long history, the organ has been predominantly used as a church instrument, though its use in secular fields has been varied – from accompanying Roman public entertainments to silent films in the 20th century. The composer most closely linked with the organ was Bach, who composed nearly 250 works for the instrument.

Brian Delf

# The saxophone

The saxophone was patented in 1846 by its inventor, Adolphe Sax. The family ranges from sopranino through soprano (left), alto and tenor (right) to the baritone. Not a member of the conventional symphony orchestra, a single saxophone sometimes appears – for example, in Walton's Belshazzar's Feast and Prokofiev's Romeo and Juliet. In such cases, either a member of the clarinet section will play the instrument or a saxophonist will be specially engaged for that performance. Recently, however, some works have been scored for more than one saxophone – Stockhausen's Carré uses alto, tenor and baritone – and if this trend were to continue, the instrument might eventually become a formal member of the orchestra. Although it has had little impact on orchestral music, the saxophone is of supreme importance to jazz and military music. The tenor was an early favourite of jazz musicians, most notably Coleman Hawkins and Lester Young, while a saxophone section is essential to the sound of the military band, heard to greatest effect in the music of John Philip Sousa.

# Early musical instruments

The history of music does not begin with the classical period, still less with the early music of Western Europe. We know that ancient civilizations made music – in some cases we have descriptions of their musical instruments and the audience's reaction, but we have little idea of what this music actually sounded like. The first music we can with some confidence reproduce is from the post-Christian era; by the 6th and 7th centuries basic methods of writing down musical notes had developed and by the 13th century notation existed much as we know it today. With a few exceptions, the earliest manuscripts of popular and secular music date from this time. Before then, knowledge of notation was confined to churchmen who had a virtual monopoly of learning. In this century, interest in this early Western music – previously dismissed as primitive – has grown apace, and with it an interest in early musical instruments.

*Musical instruments are as ancient as music – and perhaps humanity – itself, and their early history is part of myth and legend. The lyre was said to have been invented by the Greek god Hermes, and the panpipes by the god Pan. Both these instruments are undoubtedly of great antiquity, though the earliest musical instruments were probably simple members of the percussion family; it must have been very early in the evolution of humanity that someone discovered the pleasure that rhythmic, precussive sounds can produce. Until the revival of interest in early music, most of the instruments examined in the following pages were only found either in specialist museums or in the collections of a few enthusiasts. Today, the tromba marina, the sackbut, the cittern and the serpent – among many others – are commonly seen and heard in the concert hall.*

A very wide variety of percussion instruments is known to have existed in Medieval and Renaissance Europe, though unfortunately not much is known about how they were played. Most drums had heads made of animal skin stretched by rope (usually threaded through the heads) and tightened by leather thongs; and with snares stretched across the head(s). The nakers (right), predecessors of the modern timpani, were adopted in the 13th century from the Saracens by the Crusaders. They were made of copper, pottery or even wood. Hung from the player's waist, they were struck by heavy club-like beaters and were usually played in pairs. The tabor (bottom right), the most popular drum of the Middle Ages, varied in size and shape and was very commonly paired with a pipe. The rings on a triangle (centre) were a common feature right up to the 19th century. They gave off a buzzing jingle which prolonged the sound. Crotales or cymbals (behind large tabor) were usually much smaller than modern orchestral ones, of thicker metal and with deeper cups. The timbrel or tambourine came in varying sizes, and frequently had extra bells attached (below). One of the simplest percussion instruments were the clappers (below tambourine) which, like Spanish castanets, could be used for sophisticated rhythmic accompaniment or merely to scare birds in the field.

# *The lyre*

*Legend has it that Hermes stretched a piece of hide over a tortoise shell and attached strings to the cross-bar connecting the two horns jutting out from it. He presented this 'lyre' to Apollo, who became known as the god of music. Though the lyre lent its name to the 'lyric' writers of Lesbos, the Greeks did not invent the lyre. The instrument is one of the most ancient types of stringed instrument – known to have been in existence 5,000 years ago in Babylon and Egypt. Europe inherited it as an accompanying instrument from classical antiquity and Anglo-Saxon minstrels supported their recitations of the great epics and romances with instruments called* chros *or* rotta, *a modern reconstruction of which is shown below. The instrument is characterized by the cross-bar, later integrated into the arms as a continuous frame, from which strings of almost equal length wound around tuning pegs are stretched over a bridge. The tension and tuning of the strings, originally of animal gut and later of wire, are adjusted by a tuning rod. The strings are plucked unstopped – which means they can only produce a single note each – so the range of the instrument depends entirely on the number of strings. With the introduction of the bow in the 10th century, the lyre acquired a central fingerboard (right) and this form of the instrument led to the Welsh* crwth, *which survived till the beginning of the last century. Due to its unique role in giving rise to various other stringed instruments as we known them today, the lyre continued to be used as the definite symbol of music long after it had ceased to be used as a musical instrument.*

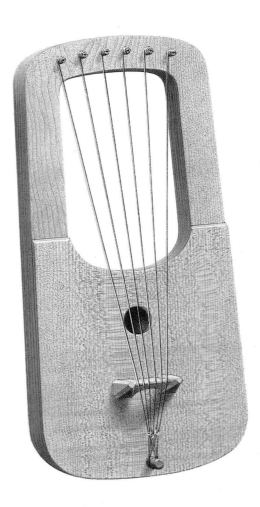

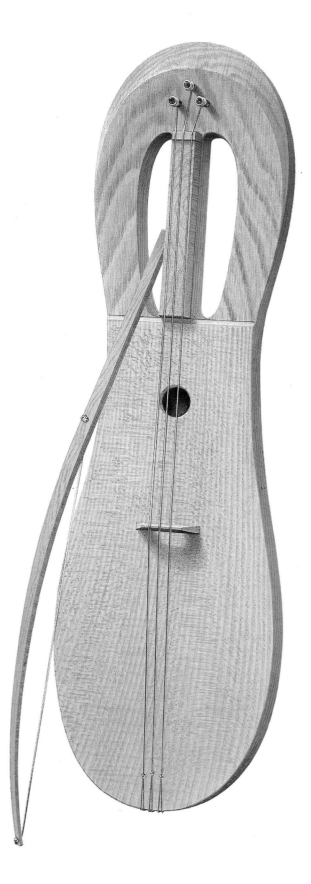

Brian Delf

# The harp

*Though we know the harp to have existed since at least 3000 BC, it was not until the Middle Ages that it achieved its pre-eminent position – principally, as a bardic instrument for accompanying all recitations of lays and sagas: which were always sung, never read. By the end of the Middle Ages, two distinct types had evolved: the Irish (right) and the Gothic (centre and left). The Irish, used by the itinerant bards at the courts of Europe, had a hollowed-out soundbox closed by a separate back; a prominent, curved forepillar and wire strings. The Gothic instrument, more indigenous to Europe, had a more slender forepillar and gut strings. The strings, which varied in number, were usually plucked with the fingernails producing a brilliant, hard tone unlike the genteel ripplings of the orchestral harp.*

*Many Gothic harps had brays – L-shaped pins which held the strings to the soundbox and could be made to vibrate against the strings, creating a strange, buzzing accompaniment. The fixed tuning of the strings severely handicapped the harp with the increasingly chromatic music of the Renaissance, and by the end of the 15th century, it had been superseded by the fretted lute. Subsequently, the harp which had once played such an important part in legend and folklore – inheriting from the lyre the role of the royal instrument of King David, and which had even been imbued with supernatural powers – became restricted to simple and traditional music.*

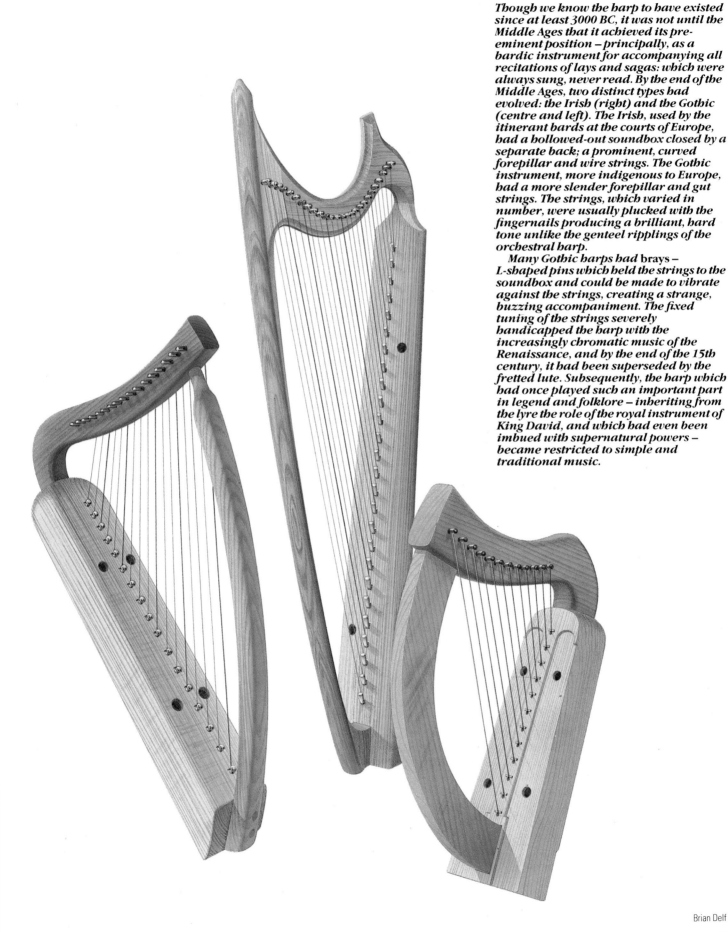

Brian Delf

# *The psaltery and the dulcimer*

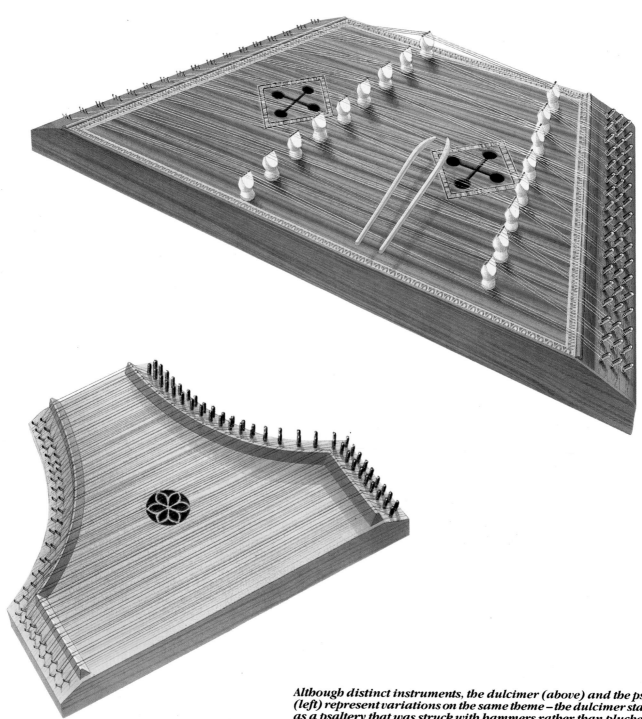

Although distinct instruments, the dulcimer (above) and the psaltery (left) represent variations on the same theme – the dulcimer started life as a psaltery that was struck with hammers rather than plucked.

The psaltery developed in the Near East. It came to Europe during the crusades, appearing in illustrations from the 12th century onwards. It took various forms, the most popular being the one which earned the name strumento di porco owing to its pig-snout appearance. It is played flat on the lap like a dulcimer, or held against the body. The dulcimer originated in Iran where it is still played today (and called the santur) and was probably brought to the west by gypsies sometime between the 12th and the 14th centuries. Both instruments consist of a flat soundbox above which open strings run from one side to the other. Being fretless, each string, or course of strings, produces only one note. The range is therefore entirely dependent on the number of strings.

Brian Delf

# The gittern

There is still some confusion about whether the gittern was the medieval precursor or northern equivalent of the guitar, or whether that role belonged to the citole, with which it is also sometimes confused. However, the popular assumption is that the instrument whose body has parallel sides, usually like a holly leaf, bears the name gittern and that the more rounded instrument was the citole. The gittern had three or four courses of gut attached at the top to a head (often shaped like an animal) and bent back from the fretted fingerboard. It was played by plucking the strings with a plectrum and used to accompany singing and dancing on all sorts of occasions. Chaucer's Miller and Pardoner both mention it in their Tales, but by the end of the 15th century, the instrument had been superseded by the lute. No music for the gittern has survived but something of its character can be deduced from the play, Ralph Roister Doister – 'Anon to our gitterne, thrumpledum, thrumpledum, thrumpledum, thrum.'

Brian Delf

# The rebec, the pochette and the medieval fiddle

These three small bowed string instruments were popular in medieval and Renaissance Europe. The eldest was the rebec (left); its sickle-shaped peg-board was a precursor of the violin. Rebecs varied in size and string number – from one to five. Played against the chest, the rebec was a minstrel's instrument for court entertainments. The pochette or kit (middle) developed from the rebec and was either pear-shaped, or in the form of a narrow boat: some were bejewelled and most had four strings. The pochette was favoured by dancing masters. The medieval fiddle (right) had a flat back and a neck distinct from its body; it contained three to five strings and was played by minstrels at entertainments and processions, and may have been a precursor of the viol.

Brian Delf

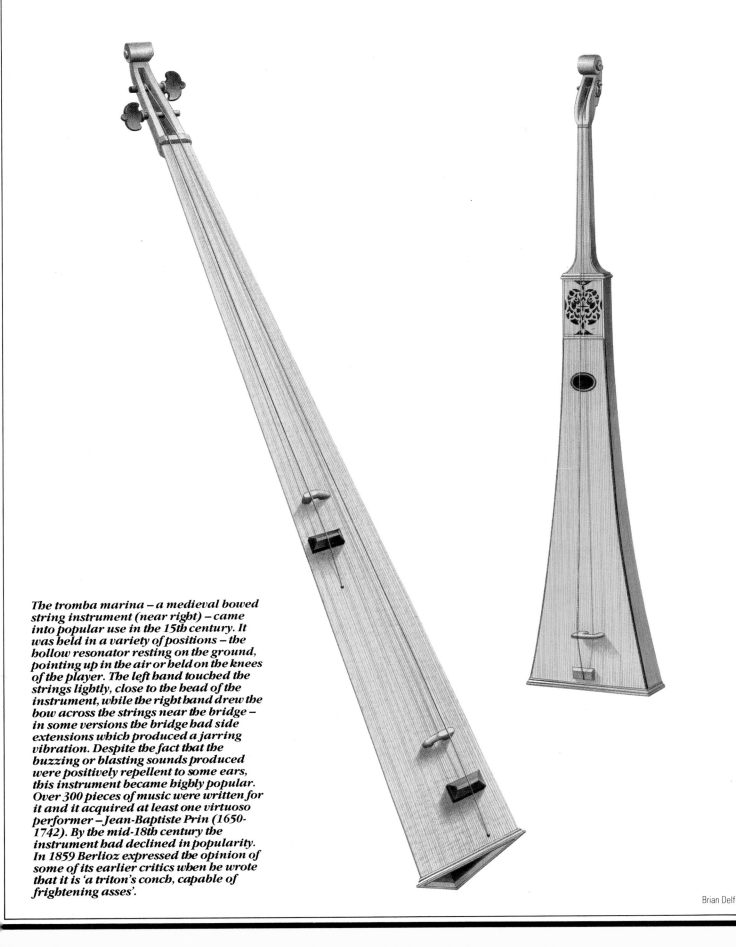

The tromba marina – a medieval bowed string instrument (near right) – came into popular use in the 15th century. It was held in a variety of positions – the hollow resonator resting on the ground, pointing up in the air or held on the knees of the player. The left hand touched the strings lightly, close to the head of the instrument, while the right hand drew the bow across the strings near the bridge – in some versions the bridge had side extensions which produced a jarring vibration. Despite the fact that the buzzing or blasting sounds produced were positively repellent to some ears, this instrument became highly popular. Over 300 pieces of music were written for it and it acquired at least one virtuoso performer – Jean-Baptiste Prin (1650-1742). By the mid-18th century the instrument had declined in popularity. In 1859 Berlioz expressed the opinion of some of its earlier critics when he wrote that it is 'a triton's conch, capable of frightening asses'.

Brian Delf

# The hurdy-gurdy

The hurdy-gurdy is an instrument of street-music. Guitar-shaped, but with no neck, it has three basic elements: a set of melody and drone strings; a resin-coated wheel (in place of a bow); and a covered keyboard. When the wheel is cranked, it rubs against the strings to produce a continuous sound. At the same time the keys, positioned below the keyboard, are depressed to bear on the melody strings. In its earliest period, the hurdy-gurdy was used in many churches and was known as the organistrum – a large, two-man instrument with a body shaped like a fiddle. By the 13th century it was also serving a secular function and had been completely altered into a small portable instrument known as the symphonia. Another two centuries elapsed, however, before it left the cloister completely and became firmly established as an instrument of wandering players. By the Renaissance, the rasping sound of the hurdy-gurdy could be heard in the courts of Europe as well as on the village green. In subsequent years, however, it was dismissed as an 'ignoble' instrument, due largely to its association with beggars and blind musicians. The 18th century saw a return to respectability, with both Haydn and Mozart composing for the hurdy-gurdy. Today it survives in countries like France and Belgium as a popular folk-music instrument.

Brian Delf

# The viol

*By the end of the 15th century bowed string instruments began to fall into two groups: the stronger-toned and brasher violins (of the unfretted lira family), which were the instruments of the professional musician; and the fretted, softer-toned instruments of the viol family, which were considered more 'noble' and used principally for domestic and amateur music-making. Viols had gut frets tied to the neck and were played held upright resting on the lap or between the knees, the bow held palm upwards so that the stronger stroke was upwards and not downwards as in the violin. Three main sizes were used in consort playing: treble (left), tenor (centre) and bass. The baryton (right) was a particularly distinct variant of the bass viol. This had six bowed strings and as many as 40 wire strings running inside the neck. These vibrated 'sympathetically' when the gut strings were bowed, though some could also be plucked independently. The baryton was popular from the mid-17th to the 18th century, especially in Germany and Austria.*

Brian Delf

# *The theorbo and the chitarrone*

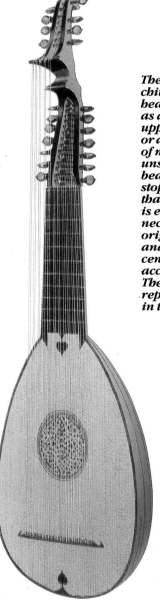

*The theorbo (left) and the chitarrone (far left) are double-headed lutes, sometimes known as archlutes. On both types the upper pegbox bears longer, bass or diapason strings – often made of metal – which were plucked unstopped. The lower pegbox bears strings which were played stopped. Both have longer necks than the lute, and the chitarrone is especially distinguished by its neck length. The instruments originated in the 16th century and were popular till the 18th century, principally as accompanying instruments. They also enjoyed a solo repertoire which was recorded in tablature.*

Brian Delf

# The colascione

The colascione was a long-necked lute
used during the 17th and 18th centuries.
Its Eastern origins are evident in its
modern counterparts, the Greek
bouzouki *and the Russian* balalaika. *Two
or three courses of strings, which were
plucked with a plectrum, were made of
metal or gut, and the soundboard was
sometimes made partially of parchment
and partially of wood. The colascione
seems to have been used with other
instruments such as the shawm, or
various percussion instruments. Because
of the limited number and the extended
length of the strings, it must have been
restricted to providing a drone
accompaniment or simple melodies.*

Brian Delf

# The cittern

The cittern is a flat-backed, metal-strung, lute-like instrument which enjoyed great popularity during the Renaissance. As a plucked instrument it was played with a quill plectrum. The strings passed over a bridge on the belly to the fingerboard. The fingerboard itself also extended onto the belly. Playing technique was just as demanding as for the lute and a large repertoire of works was written for the instrument.

Brian Delf

# The guitar

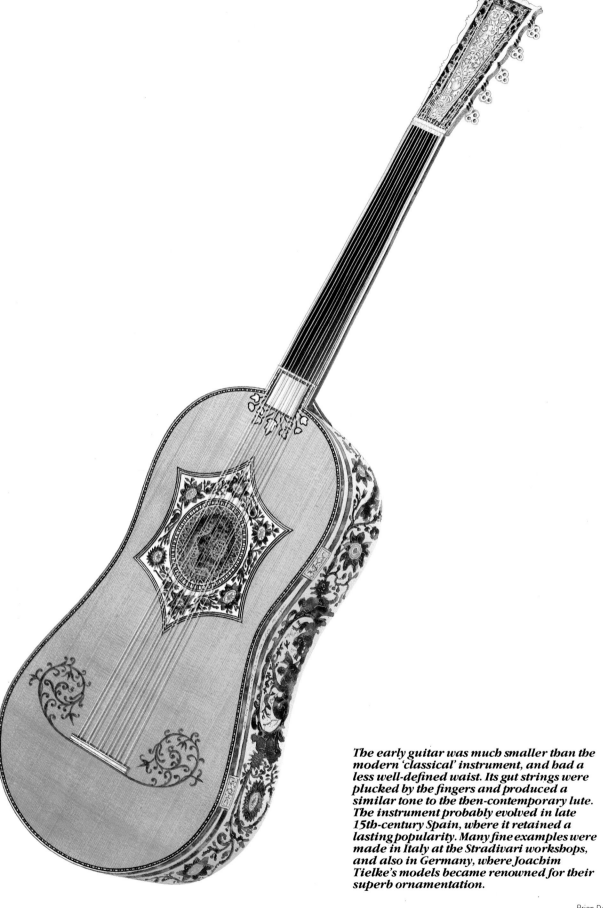

The early guitar was much smaller than the
modern 'classical' instrument, and had a
less well-defined waist. Its gut strings were
plucked by the fingers and produced a
similar tone to the then-contemporary lute.
The instrument probably evolved in late
15th-century Spain, where it retained a
lasting popularity. Many fine examples were
made in Italy at the Stradivari workshops,
and also in Germany, where Joachim
Tielke's models became renowned for their
superb ornamentation.

Brian Delf

# *The panpipes and the flute*

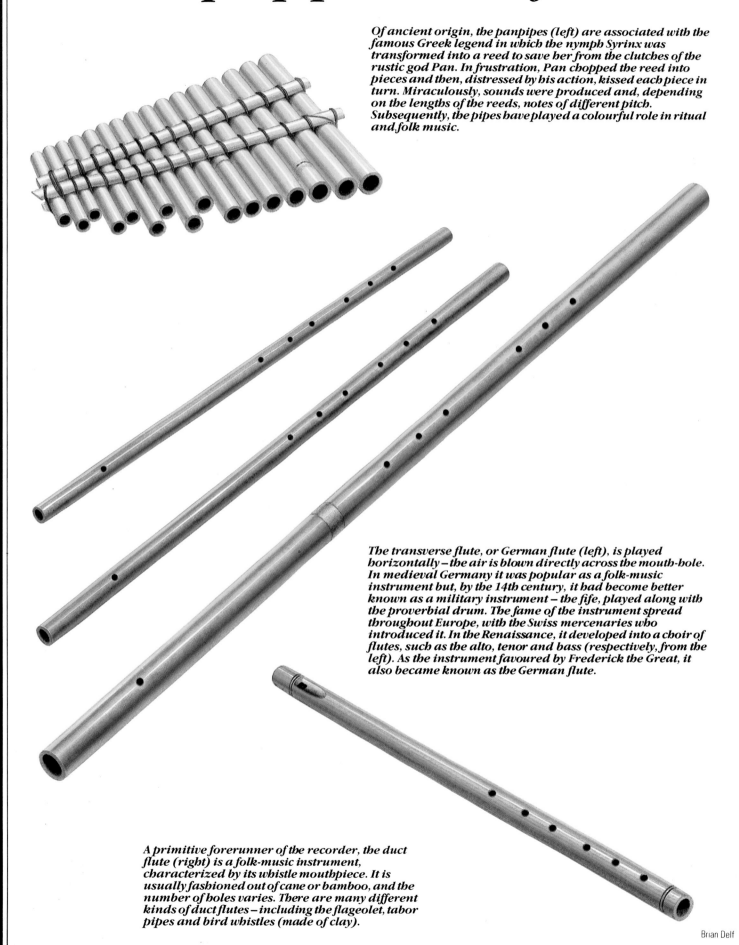

*Of ancient origin, the panpipes (left) are associated with the famous Greek legend in which the nymph Syrinx was transformed into a reed to save her from the clutches of the rustic god Pan. In frustration, Pan chopped the reed into pieces and then, distressed by his action, kissed each piece in turn. Miraculously, sounds were produced and, depending on the lengths of the reeds, notes of different pitch. Subsequently, the pipes have played a colourful role in ritual and folk music.*

*The transverse flute, or German flute (left), is played horizontally – the air is blown directly across the mouth-hole. In medieval Germany it was popular as a folk-music instrument but, by the 14th century, it had become better known as a military instrument – the fife, played along with the proverbial drum. The fame of the instrument spread throughout Europe, with the Swiss mercenaries who introduced it. In the Renaissance, it developed into a choir of flutes, such as the alto, tenor and bass (respectively, from the left). As the instrument favoured by Frederick the Great, it also became known as the German flute.*

*A primitive forerunner of the recorder, the duct flute (right) is a folk-music instrument, characterized by its whistle mouthpiece. It is usually fashioned out of cane or bamboo, and the number of holes varies. There are many different kinds of duct flutes – including the flageolet, tabor pipes and bird whistles (made of clay).*

Brian Delf

# The bagpipes

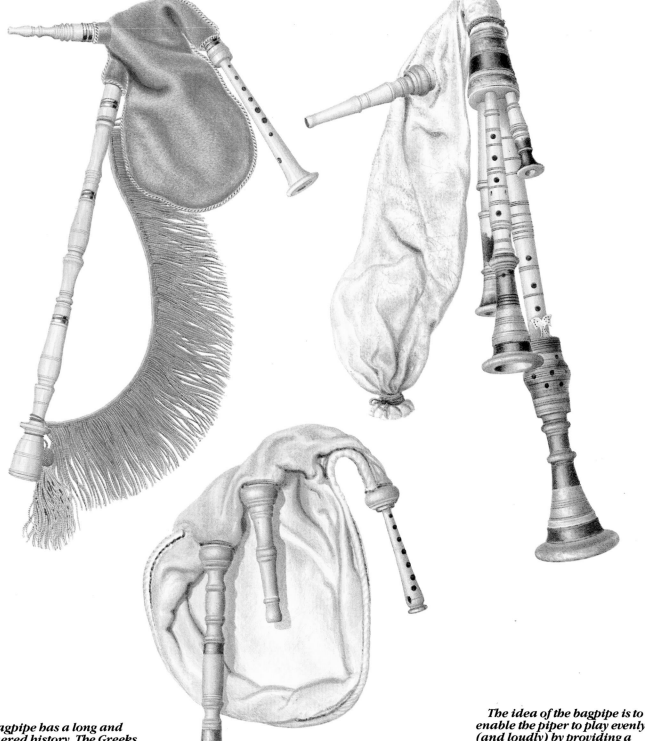

The bagpipe has a long and chequered history. The Greeks may have played them and Nero, the Emperor said to have fiddled while Rome burned, could also have provided backing on a bagpipe – he played one, too. And from the 13th century on, every folk culture in Europe seems to have had its own variant of the instrument. It reached the height of its popularity in the Middle Ages, when elaborately made instruments, such as the French musette, *accompanied courtly dances.*

Yet the bagpipe did not suit the ever more elaborate music from 1600 onwards and, therefore, declined. Leopold Mozart's The Peasant's Wedding *is one of the few classical pieces to include a part for bagpipe. Thereafter it remained largely a folk instrument, popular only on the fringes of Europe – in Italy, Spain, Brittany, Ireland and Scotland.*

The idea of the bagpipe is to enable the piper to play evenly (and loudly) by providing a reservoir of air, the skin bag. The piper fills the bag through a blowpipe *and squeezes air out through a reed into a* chanter, a tube drilled with holes to vary the pitch. But there are many variations, notably those with drones *which play no part in the melody but fill out the sound. The illustration shows just three of the local variations: the Spanish* gaita *(left); the Breton* biniou *(centre); and the Italian* zampogna *(right).*

Brian Delf

# The gemshorn, the horn and the oliphant

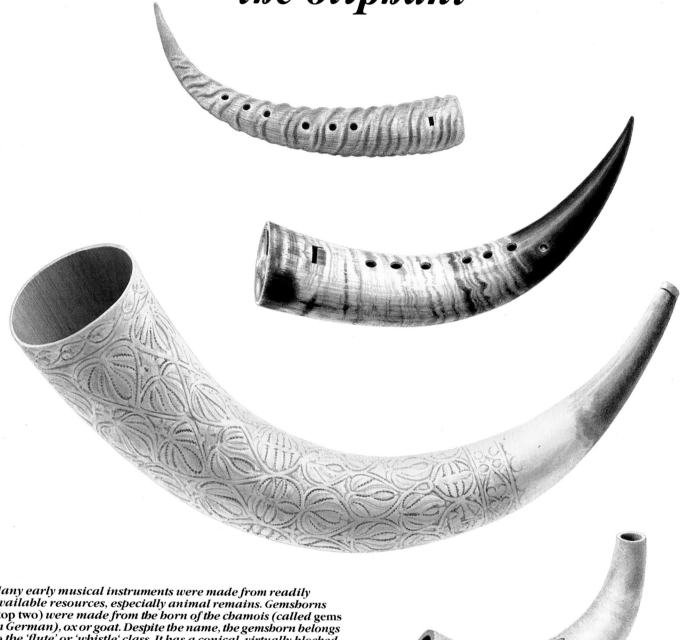

Many early musical instruments were made from readily available resources, especially animal remains. Gemshorns (top two) were made from the horn of the chamois (called gems in German), ox or goat. Despite the name, the gemshorn belongs to the 'flute' or 'whistle' class. It has a conical, virtually blocked-up bore; finger holes and a vent hole. It is blown from the wide end, producing a sweet, soft and somewhat watery tone with great transmitting power and not unlike that of an ocarina or a recorder, of which it may well be a true precursor. Since it tones well with the human voice, it was used to accompany carols and madrigals, but was also played for medieval and early Renaissance dance and ranged in size from very large bass instruments to much smaller descant ones.

Animal horns had been used as signalling instruments. Blown through the narrower end or sometimes through an added mouthpiece – the characteristic of the 'horn' or 'trumpet' class – they produced blasts of varying degrees. By the 10th century, finger holes were added (bottom) allowing for simple melodies. Ceremonial instruments, intricately carved and sometimes from elephant tusks, were called oliphants (centre). Used as regalia, they were imbued with great symbolic and magical potency. Charlemagne is said to have heard Roland's call for help from several miles, but in vain, as the wounded hero had burst both the instrument and an artery in his neck with the fatal attempt to blow it.

Brian Delf

# The cornett and the serpent

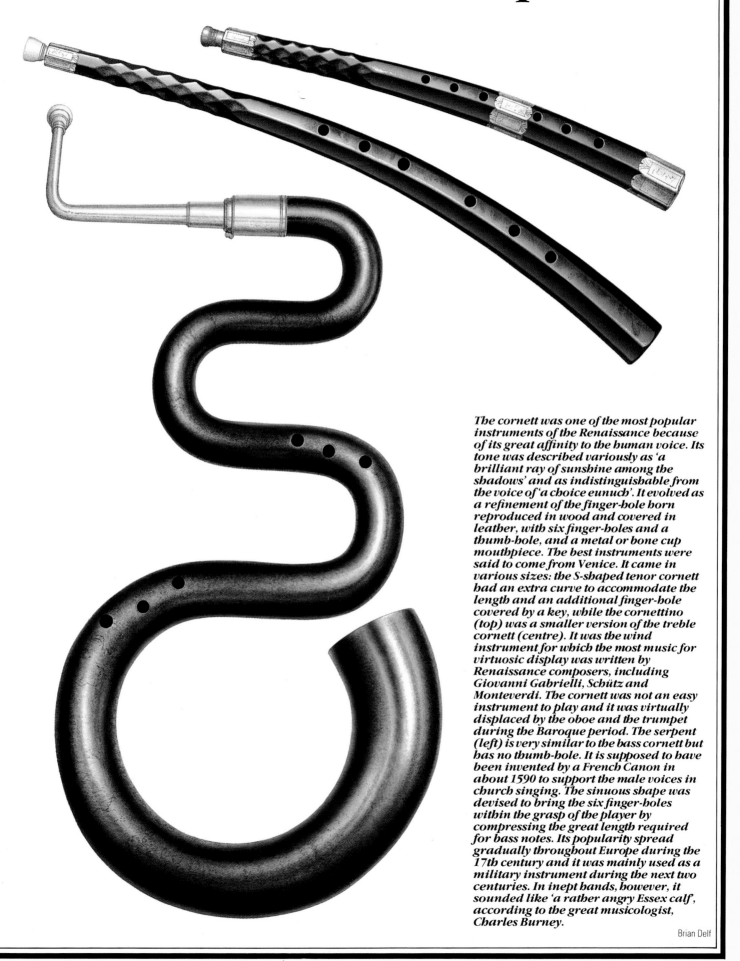

The cornett was one of the most popular instruments of the Renaissance because of its great affinity to the human voice. Its tone was described variously as 'a brilliant ray of sunshine among the shadows' and as indistinguishable from the voice of 'a choice eunuch'. It evolved as a refinement of the finger-hole horn reproduced in wood and covered in leather, with six finger-holes and a thumb-hole, and a metal or bone cup mouthpiece. The best instruments were said to come from Venice. It came in various sizes: the S-shaped tenor cornett had an extra curve to accommodate the length and an additional finger-hole covered by a key, while the cornettino (top) was a smaller version of the treble cornett (centre). It was the wind instrument for which the most music for virtuosic display was written by Renaissance composers, including Giovanni Gabrielli, Schütz and Monteverdi. The cornett was not an easy instrument to play and it was virtually displaced by the oboe and the trumpet during the Baroque period. The serpent (left) is very similar to the bass cornett but has no thumb-hole. It is supposed to have been invented by a French Canon in about 1590 to support the male voices in church singing. The sinuous shape was devised to bring the six finger-holes within the grasp of the player by compressing the great length required for bass notes. Its popularity spread gradually throughout Europe during the 17th century and it was mainly used as a military instrument during the next two centuries. In inept hands, however, it sounded like 'a rather angry Essex calf', according to the great musicologist, Charles Burney.

Brian Delf

# *The trumpet and the sackbut*

*A long, virtually cylindrical instrument with a flared bell, the
early trumpet was used mainly for military and ceremonial
purposes. By the 15th century, improved techniques in
metalworking allowed the trumpet to be folded (top). With
their flamboyant banners and fanfares, the trumpeteers
formed an élite corps within a sovereign's retinue; later
trumpeteers grouped together in exclusive guilds, and
specialized in difficult techniques of performing – Bach
provided them with some opportunities for virtuosic display
in his second Brandenburg concerto. By the mid-15th
century, the trumpet had acquired a movable slide which
allowed the length of the tube to be varied greatly. An early
trombone, the sackbut (above) was used especially to
accompany singing, thanks to its improved and more
accurate range and adaptability.*

Brian Delf

# *The shawm*

One of the most common and characteristic musical sounds of the Middle Ages and the Renaissance was that produced by the shawm. Imported from the Arabs in the 13th century, its piercing tone and volume, which was due to its conical bore, is said to have scared the Crusaders. The double reed in the soprano and tenor instruments (three on the left) is fitted into a conical metal tube called the staple. This, in turn, is partly covered by a 'piouette', and gives the lips support while blasting the air through. In the bass instruments (two on the right) the reed is inserted into a bent tube, the crook. Like the recorder, a metal key covers the bottommost hole and, in turn, is covered by a decorated 'fontanelle'.

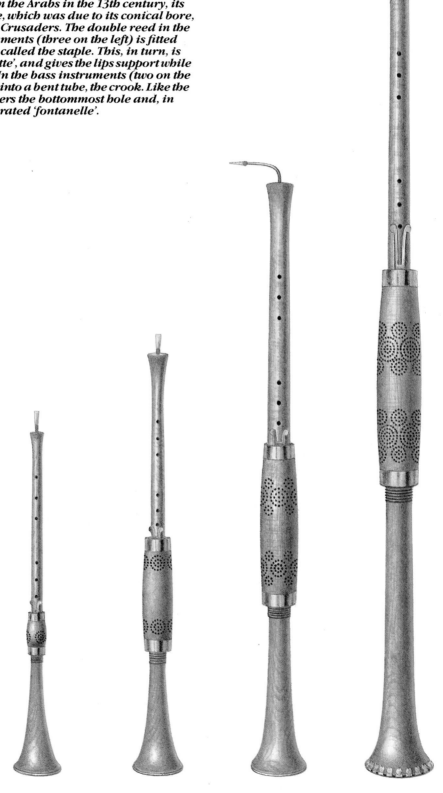

Brian Delf

# *The recorder*

The recorder was for long the most common and prominent of woodwind instruments. Basically a duct flute with seven finger holes and a thumb hole, it was developed from the medieval pipe. There were several sizes, from bass instruments with brass crooks to shrill descant ones – including tenor and alto instruments – to enable consort playing. Renaissance instruments (two on the right) were made in one piece, and in the larger sizes the seventh hole was often covered by a key which was partially hidden by a movable barrel with perforations. The Baroque version (two on the left) was invented in the mid-17th century and made in three sections. By turning the sections, the length could be adjusted for tuning. Fine specimens, often with ivory moulding, were made in the French workshops of Hotteterre and Bressan.

Both Bach and Handel wrote music for solo recorder, but the instrument's inability to fluctuate volume without distorting pitch handicapped it for the more expressive music of the Classical age. It was superseded by the flute, only to regain popularity in modern times.

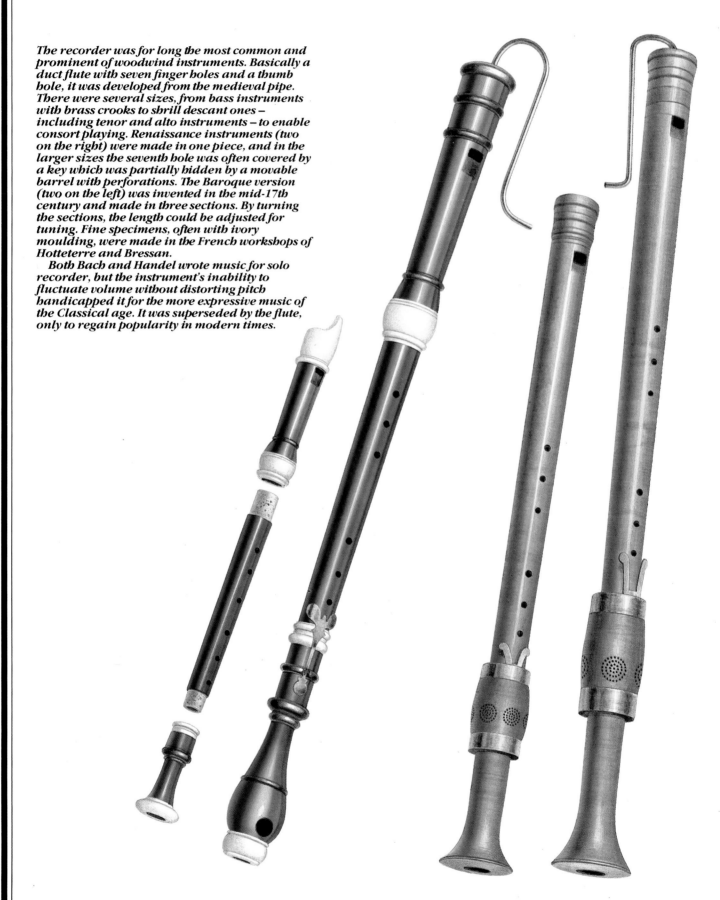

Brian Delf

# The crumhorn

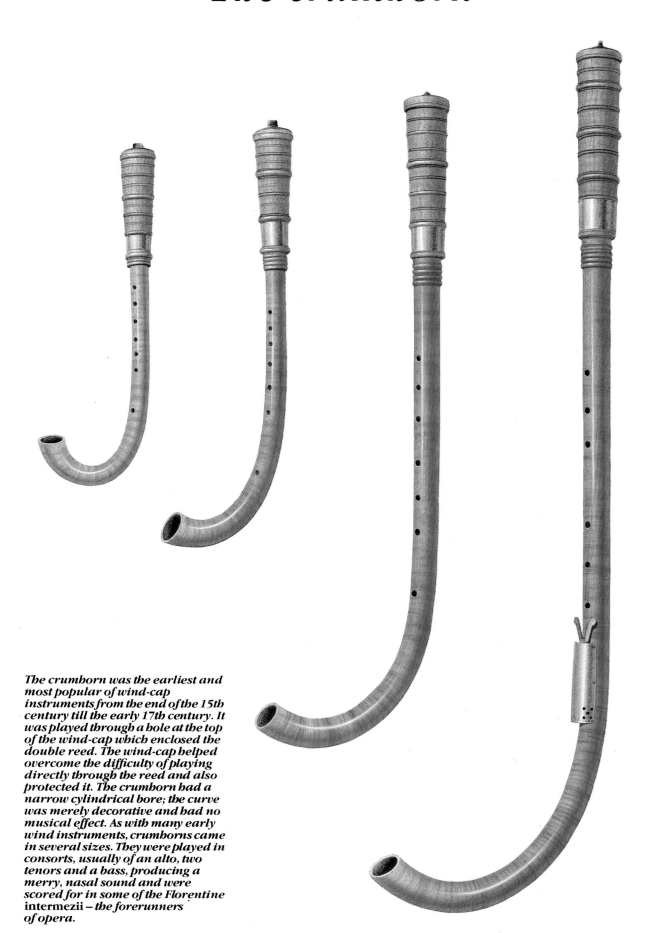

The crumhorn was the earliest and most popular of wind-cap instruments from the end of the 15th century till the early 17th century. It was played through a hole at the top of the wind-cap which enclosed the double reed. The wind-cap helped overcome the difficulty of playing directly through the reed and also protected it. The crumhorn had a narrow cylindrical bore; the curve was merely decorative and had no musical effect. As with many early wind instruments, crumhorns came in several sizes. They were played in consorts, usually of an alto, two tenors and a bass, producing a merry, nasal sound and were scored for in some of the Florentine intermezii – the forerunners of opera.

Brian Delf

# *The curtal, the rackett and the sordun*

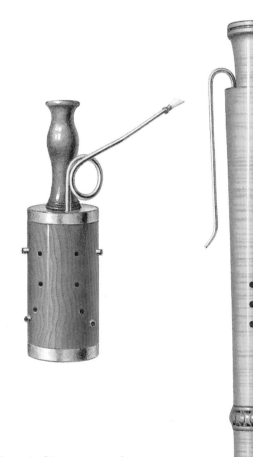
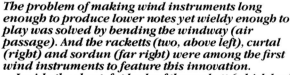

*The problem of making wind instruments long enough to produce lower notes yet wieldy enough to play was solved by bending the windway (air passage). And the racketts (two, above left), curtal (right) and sordun (far right) were among the first wind instruments to feature this innovation.*

*Inside the short, fat body of the rackett (which had finger-holes on the side) were several short parallel bores connected to each other to form a windway nearly a metre long. The rackett was played through a double reed, either enclosed in an ivory pirouette (left) or inserted into a coiled crook (second, left), with the windway opening out below and above the body respectively.*

*The curtal was a late 16th-century Italian invention and, with its two interconnected bores, was similar to the bassoon. The crook was inserted into the narrower bore while the wider one ended in a flare at the top. An open key was protected by a brass cover.*

*The sordun had a narrow, cylindrical windway running down and up inside the wooden column, terminating at the top, and was used in ensembles of mixed wind instruments.*

Brian Delf

# The chalumeau and the bassett horn

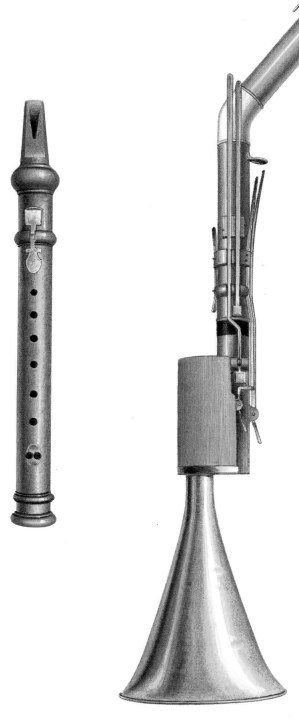

The cylindrical-bored chalumeau (left) was an early form of the clarinet, with the mouthpiece slit to form the single reed. It appeared towards the end of the 17th century and Handel and Telemann were among those who scored for it in 18th-century operas. The bassett horn (right) was similar in pitch to the alto clarinet, but had an extended range – an advantage it held over all other clarinets. The brass bell was often flattened to fit between the knees and the 'box' above it contained three parallel and inter-connected air channels. Invented in the 17th century, it assumed many different shapes and its slightly dour tone inspired Mozart's masonic music.

Brian Delf

# *The virginal*

DVM VIXI TACVI

MORTVA DVLCE CANO

AVRES ANIMI FORES

*The virginal belongs to the harpsichord family of plucked keyboard instruments, but its characteristic box-like shape is due to the strings running parallel to the keyboard instead of away from it. The longer bass strings are at the front, the shorter treble ones at the back, and all are stretched over two bridges.*

*The jacks, which pluck the strings, run diagonally from the shortest for the bass at the left to the longer for the treble at the right. The virginal was often confused with other plucked keyboard instruments such as the spinet and the harpsichord; the origins of the instrument's name remain obscure (but there is no association with Elizabeth I the Virgin Queen). Two types were prominent – the Italian and the Flemish, the latter having a recessed keyboard, a vaulted lid and paper pattern decoration (left). This model was also most popular in 16th-century England where composers such as William Byrd, John Bull, Giles Farnaby and Orlando Gibbons wrote copious anthologies of music for the virginal, heralding the Golden Age of English music.*

Brian Delf

The spinet is a member of the
harpsichord family. For many
years, the name was used
interchangeably with the virginal
but the shape is distinctly
different. Unlike the virginal, the
strings run at an angle to the
keyboard and not parallel to it,
nor away from it as in the
harpsichord. The name derives
from the Latin spina (thorn) as,
like the harpsichord and the
virginal, the strings are plucked by
a quilled jack.

Brian Delf

# The clavichord

The clavichord, a smaller and cheaper keyboard instrument than the harpsichord, had become, by the 18th century, the most important instrument in domestic use. Though it never attained the more public tones of the harpsichord, unlike that instrument it could sustain notes and graduate its volume, and it thus emerged as the more expressive of the two. The strings were not plucked but were instead hit by a tangent (a brass blade) at the end of the key. The clavichord did not require as many strings as it had keys, as several tangents could hit the same string at different places – a factor which contributed greatly to its small size, portability and easy tuning.

Brian Delf

# Glossary

# A

**abstract (or absolute) music** Music written for its own sake rather than to illustrate a (non-musical) idea or theme. It is the opposite of *programme* music, such as Beethoven's 'Pastoral' Symphony which seeks to convey aspects of rural life through music. In Germany, though, the term is used to describe music which is dull and academic.

**a cappella** Means, literally, in chapel style, but it has come to mean unaccompanied part singing.

**accelerando** Getting gradually quicker.

**accidental** Sign indicating that a single note is played sharper or flatter than normal for the key of the piece.

**accompagnato** Short for *recitativo accompagnato* which means that the accompaniment must follow the singer, allowing the singer to vary the tempo at will.

**acoustics** Relating to sound. It has a number of applications. The science of *acoustics* is the physics of sound. The *acoustics* of a building or concert hall are the way physical layout affects the way we hear music. An *acoustic guitar* does not need artificial amplification to be adequately heard.

**ad libitum** Often abbreviated to ad lib. At will. Where marked in a piece of music, the performer can vary the tempo or the instrumentation at will, or improvise for the period indicated.

**adagietto** Either: slow but not as slow as *adagio,* or a short *adagio* composition.

**adagio** Played slowly, though not so slowly as *largo.*

**affettuoso** Tenderly, affectionately. Also 'affected', mannered.

**agitato** Excited, fast tempo.

**Agnus Dei** Lamb of God. Part of the Latin Church Mass. In musical setting of the Mass, the *agnus dei* is usually the last or last but one section.

**agogic** Notes accentuated not by the force with which they are played but by the time for which they are held.

**air** Gentle tune or song, or simply a melodic composition such as Bach's 'Air on a G String'.

**Alberti bass** Simple bass accompaniment in keyboard music, where the left hand plays the notes of a chord rhythmically in the following order: lowest; highest; middle; highest. Named after Italian keyboard player Domenico Alberti.

**aleatory** A piece in which the composition or the performance may vary by chance. The ad lib passages of Baroque keyboard pieces are aleatory. So are the modern compositions decided by a throw of a dice.

**allegretto** Fast and lively, but not as fast as *allegro.*

**allegro** Fast and lively. The first movement of sonatas are often played *allegro.* So the first movement form is sometimes called *sonata allegro.*

**allemande** A French word meaning 'German'. It has two meanings in music. **1.** A slow dance in common time. It originated in Germany, but during the Baroque period (1600–1750), it became established as the first movement of the *suite.* **2.** South German folk dance similar to the waltz.

**alto** High. The alto is the highest adult male voice, usually produced by singing *falsetto.* The lowest female voice is the *contralto.*

**andante** Usually used to indicate a piece of music played at a medium tempo, or 'walking pace'.

**answer** See *fugue.*

**anthem** A national song. Also, a choral piece sung at a religious service.

**anticipation** A note which is sounded before the chord to which it belongs, creating dissonance with the preceding chord.

**antiphon** A religious chant. A biblical extract set to music.

**appassionata** Impassioned – an instruction to the musician. Also used to describe Beethoven's Piano Sonata in F minor.

**appogiatura** A musical character written before the main note which steals the emphasis from it and effectively halves its time value.

**arabesque** A short piece of music which is elaborately decorative.

**aria** Music written for a solo vocalist with instrumental accompaniment, particularly associated with opera.

**arpeggio** The notes of a chord played one after the other rather than simultaneously.

**arrangement** A piece of music adapted so that it can be played by an instrument for which it was not originally composed.

**atonality** Describes music composed in no definite key.

**attacca** Attack or begin. A direction to the musician to continue from one section of the music to the next without pause.

**augmentation** The process of extending the length of note to prolong a musical phrase or melody. An *augmented interval* is one that has been increased by a semitone.

**ayre** A composition written for several voices, often without musical accompaniment. It was very popular in England around 1600.

# B

**badinerie, badinage** A term used to refer to a piece of music with a playful mood.

**bagatelle** A short, light-hearted composition, usually written for the piano.

**balalaika** Russian triangular instrument, similar to a guitar, but usually with only three strings.

**ballabile** 'Dance-like', a term often used in opera.

**ballad** A traditional folk song, passed down through generations. The words usually tell a story.

**ballade** A long romantic instrumental piece, usually written for the piano.

**ballet** A spectacular, form of dance, with an orchestral accompaniment.

**band** A large group of instrumental players, usually used to describe a combination of brass and percussion instruments.

**bar** (In the USA, a *measure.*) A metrical division of musical time. When written, nearly all music with a regular rhythm is divided into small sections, marked off by vertical lines across the stave. A 'bar' is one small section. The line marking it off is a bar-line.

**barcarolle** A Venetian boatman's song or a composition with a slow swinging rhythm.

**baritone 1** Male voice with a range in between bass and tenor. **2** Instrument with range below the 'tenor', e.g. baritone saxophone.

**Baroque music** Music from the period roughly 1600–1750, named after the elaborate, highly ornamented style of architecture popular in Germany and Austria at the time.

**baryton** A type of bass viol popular in the 18th century. Haydn wrote many baryton compositions for his patron Prince Nikolaus Esterházy.

**bass 1** The lowest part in a musical arrangement or, simply, low notes. **2** The deepest male voice, sometimes divided into *basso profondo* (very deep) and *basso cantant* ('singing'). **3** The lowest of many types of instrument.

**bassoon** One of the deepest and biggest of the orchestral woodwind instruments. Like the *oboe,* it has a double reed.

**baton** Stick used by the conductor to beat time.

**battaglia** A piece of music describing a battle. There are many famous battaglia, from William Byrd's *The Battell* (1591) through to Tchaikovsky's *'1812' Overture.*

**battery 1** The percussion section of the orchestra. **2** The way chords in Baroque music were often played as arpeggios.

**beat** The basic rhythmic pulse of music.

**beats** When the vibrations from two strings of a musical instrument coincide, they reinforce each other to create 'beats'. These beats can be used as an aid to tuning the instrument.

**bel canto** Literally meaning 'beautiful singing', this word was adopted in the middle of the 19th century to describe the light, elegant style of singing popular in Italian operas of the previous century. Since then, however, it has tended to be used for any singing style that the person using the word finds attractive.

**Benedictus** In musical settings of the Latin mass, the Benedictus usually followed the Sanctus. In the Renaissance, the Benedictus was usually set for fewer voices than the rest of the mass. Later, Bach used it as a solo, while Mozart and Haydn set it for solo and choirs.

**berceuse** A lullaby, usually for solo piano, in gentle 6/8 time. Chopin's op. 57 is the most famous example.

**bergamasca** Lively Italian peasant dance dating from around 1600. It is referred to as a 'bergomask' in Shakespeare's *A Midsummer Night's Dream*.

**binary form** A basic musical form in which the music is made up of two main parts, A and B, which are usually repeated AABB. Binary form was very popular in dances of the Baroque period, but it was used well before that and is still widely used today. The Italian keyboard player, Domenico Scarlatti (1685–1757), wrote binary form variations which provided the basis for sonata form music.

**bitonality** Referring to music written in two different keys at once. Popular with American Charles Ives and French composers of the early 20th century.

**blues** A slow and melancholy but rhythmic form of black American folk song. Its influence on popular western music from jazz to rock has been enormous. Even 'classical' composers such as George Gershwin, have fallen under the spell of the blues.

**bocca chiusa** Italian term for closed mouth, it is a wordless humming or singing with the mouth closed but the teeth slightly parted. It is used particularly in modern choral music.

**bolero** A Spanish dance in triple rhythm for pairs of dancers who usually accompany themselves with singing and castanets.

**bouche fermée** French term for closed mouth. See *bocca chiusa* above.

**bourrée** Can refer either to a French folk dance or a court dance which was most popular from the mid-17th to the mid-18th century in France.

**brace** The bracket joining musical staves together at the left-hand side; it indicates that the notes on the staves should be played together.

**brass** This is the collective name given to wind instruments originally made of brass, but which now may be made of other metals, and which are blown through a cup-shaped or funnel-shaped mouthpiece. Saxophones have reed mouthpieces and are therefore not included in this group. The main brass instruments played in an orchestra are the horn, trumpet, trombone and tuba.

**bravura** The Italian word means literally 'skill' or 'bravery' but when it is used to describe a musical performance it implies a bold and striking, even swaggering display of technique. The term was common in the 18th century where the *aria di bravura* was one which made great demands on the singer's technical abilities.

**break 1.** The term can be used to refer to the change in tone quality as either voices or wind instruments pass between different registers. **2.** It can also refer to a short, usually improvised solo in a jazz piece which gives the performer a chance to demonstrate his musical skills. **3.** It describes the permanent change in range and quality which takes place in a boy's voice at puberty.

**breve** (In the USA a **double whole note**.) Originally the short note in music, it has now come to be the longest as longer notes have fallen out of use and shorter ones have been introduced. Its time value is equivalent to two semibreves. (In America the semibreve is considered to be a whole note.)

**bridge 1.** The specially shaped piece of wood that supports the strings in stringed instruments and transmits their vibrations to the body of the instrument. **2.** A short passage which links two main sections of composition together.

**brilliant, brillante** An instruction to play with great verve or in a sparkling way. It usually applies to solo performances.

**brio** An Italian word meaning dash or spirit. The instruction to play *con brio* means to play with vigour.

**brisé** The French for broken, it is applied to a chord played in an *arpeggio* fashion, that is with the notes played in sequence rather than simultaneously. The term is also used for string music played with detached, short movements.

**broken chord** Notes are played successively rather than simultaneously, and in any order.

**broken consort** An old English term for a group of different kinds of instrument.

**bruscamente** An Italian term meaning play brusquely or in a rather offhand manner.

**brustwerk** A German word for a separate group of organ pipes usually with its own manual and with a softer registration than the main group of pipes of *Hauptwerk*. It is usually situated at the front of the instrument just above the keyboard.

**buffo, buffa** The Italian for 'comic' often used in opera to describe singing parts. Opera buffo means literally 'comic opera'.

**bugle** A brass or copper type of horn still widely used by armies in many countries today. The instrument consists of a cup-shaped mouthpiece, a conical tube and a bell. As it has no valves only a few notes of the harmonic scale can be played on it. A version of the bugle was common in medieval times as a hunting horn. Later it was used for military signalling and, of course, in military bands.

**bull roarer** Also known as a thunderstick or whizzer, it is an instrument found among primitive peoples such as Australian aborigines or the American Indians. An object such as a thin, flat piece of wood is swung on the end of a string to produce a whirring sound. Changes in pitch are produced by varying the speed of rotation.

**burletta** An Italian term to describe an operatic comedy or musical farce.

**Byzantine music** This is the name for the Christian liturgical chant of the Eastern Orthodox Church. Some of it dates back as far as the early 4th century to the time when Constantinople was founded on the site of the ancient city of Byzantium.

# C

**cabaletta** A short aria or passage in a song characterized by repeats. It is also used to describe the final, fast section of certain 19th century arias or duets.

**cadence** A progression of chords which marks the end of a phrase, movement or piece of music.

**cadenza** A passage, originally improvised, which is inserted between the chords of the final cadence of a piece, to enable a singer or solo instrumentalist to display skill and virtuosity. Now many composers write their own cadenzas.

**caelsura** A momentary pause in the music.

**calando** The Italian word which means 'becoming quieter' is used to indicate that the music should lessen in volume and sometimes, also, slow in tempo.

**calypso** A style of Caribbean dance, music and song which has evolved from African and West Indian folk-music. The lyrics usually provide humorous or satirical comment on current events or personalities. Calypsos can be played on ordinary dance band instruments but more typically by steel bands.

**cambiare** The Italian for 'to change', this is sometimes used as an orchestral instruction, for example for a woodwind player to change to a different instrument.

**camera, da** This Italian term means literally 'for the small room' and is applied to a type of music or a musical group suited to a small gathering in intimate surroundings.

**campana, campane** The Italian for 'bell, bells', which may be used in an orchestra. 'Campanella' means 'little bell' and plural 'campanelle' is sometimes used for glockenspiel.

**campanology** The art of bell ringing.

**can can** A lively dance in 2/4 time. It became famous for its daring in the Paris music halls of the 1830s and has inspired various composers including Offenbach who used it in his *Orpheus in the Underworld*.

**cancrizans** This term refers to a passage in a composition in which the theme is repeated backwards. A canon cancrizans is one in which the imitating voice sings the notes in reverse order to those of the first voice.

**canon** This is a composition or part of a composition in which one strand of melody, either sung, or played on an instrument, provides the rule, which others imitate exactly, note for note at intervals, so that overlapping results. One of the best known forms of canon is the *round*. One such is *Frère Jacques*.

**cantabile** Italian word meaning in a singing, flowing manner. It is used as an instruction to indicate that playing should bring out the singing, melodic quality of the piece.

**cantata** The Italian means 'sung piece' and a cantata is a work composed for one or more voices, usually with orchestral accompaniment.

**cantatrice** Italian for a female singer.

**canticle** A hymn with biblical words, other than those from the Psalms, used in Christian worship.

**cantilena** An Italian word used to indicate a smooth, flowing, melodic instrumental or vocal line.

**canto** The Italian for 'song' or 'melody'. The instruction *col canto* means that the accompanist should take his time from the performer of the melody.

**cantor** This is the name given in Jewish and early Christian worship to the person leading the singing. In the Lutheran Church the term referred to the director of music. J S Bach was Cantor of St Thomas's, Leipzig.

**cantus firmus** The term means 'fixed melody' and is usually applied to a melody borrowed from another source and used as the basis of the work, with other melodies being set in *counterpoint* against it.

**canzona, canzone** This Italian word for 'song, songs', was applied in the 16th century to popular poems and songs set to music. It can also refer to instrumental pieces which developed from or were influenced by vocal works.

**canzonet, canzonette** A name for a light, simple song.

**cappella** The Italian for 'chapel'. The term *a cappella* describes choral music which is performed unaccompanied.

**capriccio/caprice** Various types of light, humorous and quick music. The term refers to the mood of the performer rather than the structure of the music.

**carillon** Continental church bells that are normally housed in a tower or high outdoor frame and operated by wires or levers.

**castanet** Percussion instrument consisting of two wooden shells clicked together by the fingers. When used in orchestras, castanets are usually mounted on a small stick so that they can be shaken together more conveniently.

**castrato** Male singer who had his sexual organs modified before puberty to facilitate the development of a powerful voice in the soprano or contralto range. Opera roles intended for castrati are now generally sung by sopranos.

**catch** A type of 'round' song for unaccompanied voices, in which each voice sings exactly the same melody but enters at a different time. Typically, a catch is a round with humorous words.

**cavatina** A short aria, consisting of one section instead of the usual three. Also, a slow, song-like and generally short instrumental piece.

**cédez** A French direction meaning 'give way' to indicate that the speed should be diminished.

**celeste** A 19th-century keyboard instrument that produces a bell-like sound. Tchaikovsky used a celeste in his *Nutcracker* ballet.

**cello** From violoncello, the bass member of the violin family and a favourite solo instrument since the 18th century.

**chamber music** Intimate ensemble music, as distinct from, say, solo or orchestral music, originally intended for domestic and private, and frequently amateur, performance. The principal form of chamber music is the string quartet.

**chamber opera** A small-scale opera.

**chamber orchestra** A small orchestra capable of playing in a room or small hall.

**chamber symphony** A small-scale symphony designed for a few players.

**change ringing** An English ring of church bells may consist of any number from five to 20. With five bells, 120 variations of order, or *changes,* are possible. Change ringing is a popular pastime and standard changes are known by traditional names such as 'Grandsire Triples'.

**changed note** The English for *nota cambiata,* a device in strict counterpoint by which a non-harmonic note is used on an accented beat.

**chanson** Lyric compositions set to French words, particularly medieval and Renaissance French songs for several voices.

**characteristic piece** Music representative of a mood, place etc. Sometimes applied by composers to short instrumental works, usually for piano solos.

**chest of viols** Any complete set of viols of different sizes, usually six instruments.

**chest voice** The lowest register of the voice that is felt by the singer to be coming from the chest.

**chiuso** A way of modifying or 'stopping' a horn note by placing a hand in its bell.

**choir** A group of singers, especially in a church. Also an abbreviation for *choir-organ,* a division of an organ with mainly soft stops suitable for accompanying choirs.

**choral** Music sung by a choir or chorus.

**choral symphony** Either a symphony that includes a chorus or a work of symphonic dimensions for voices alone.

**chorale** A type of traditional German hymn-tune for congregational use, of which Martin Luther wrote many. A *chorale-prelude* is an instrumental piece (usually for organ) based on a chorale.

**chord** Any simultaneous combination of notes; sometimes refers strictly to any simultaneous combination of not less than three notes.

**choreography** The art of arranging dances, especially ballet.

**chorus** A group of singers singing the same part, as opposed to soloists. Also the refrain of a song or a group of instruments used in the same way as a human chorus.

**chromatic** A form of scale in which all the intervals between notes are a semitone. From the Greek word for colour (*chroma*).

**cittern** A plucked wire-strung instrument with a pear-shaped body and a flat back. The cittern (also *cither, cithern*) was extensively used for popular music from the 16th to the 18th century.

**clarinet** Woodwind instrument with single reed and usually a wooden body in use since the mid-18th century. The modern system of keys was developed in the 1840s.

**classical/classicism** Refers vaguely to art music as opposed to popular music and (as in *Classical/Classicism*) strictly to music of the period *c.* 1750–1830 embracing the development of the classical symphony and concerto by composers such as Haydn, Mozart and Beethoven.

**clavichord** A soft-toned keyboard instrument which was very popular as a solo instrument from the 16th to the 18th century and was revived in the 20th century for old music.

**clavier** Originally a French term meaning a keyboard or manual (of an organ) but in German its meaning was extended to include piano or any keyboard instrument. Today it is used as a general term for keyboard instruments, as in J. S. Bach's, *The Well-Tempered Clavier.*

**clef** A sign that fixes the location of a particular note on the staff, and so the location of all other notes. For example, the treble clef fixes the note middle C on the line below the staff.

**close harmony** Harmony in which the notes of a chord lie near each other.

**cluster** A group of adjacent notes on the piano keyboard sounded together.

**coda** The Italian for 'tail', a coda is a section of a movement considered to be added on to the end as a rounding-off device rather than a structural necessity.

**codetta** A 'little tail'. Does for a section of a movement what a *coda* does for a movement.

**col legno** From the Italian and meaning 'with the wood', this is an instruction to players of bowed instruments (violins, etc.) to strike the strings with the stick of the bow rather than the hair, producing a dry, staccato sound.

**coloratura** A florid style of singing, particularly by very high soprano voices in opera.

**combination tone** The sound produced when two loud notes are sounded simultaneously, which is not present when either of them is sounded separately. Sometimes called *resultant tone.*

**come** The Italian for 'like' or 'as'. The frequently used phrase *come prima* means 'as at first', the phrase *come sopra,* 'as above', and *come sta,* means 'as it stands'.

**commodo or comodo** An Italian word meaning 'easy' or 'comfortably', so *tempo comodo* means 'at a moderate speed'.

**common chord** Also known as a triad, this is a three-note chord which consists of a particular note played together with the third and fifth above. For example CEG is the common chord of C Major.

**common metre** Sometimes referred to as 'ballad metre' this is the metre of the usual four-line hymn verse with alternate lines of 8 and 6 syllables.

**common time** Another name for 4/4 time where there are four crotchets to the bar.

**compass** The range that can be produced by any instrument or voice from the highest to the lowest note. With brass, wind or stringed instruments the lowest note is fixed but the higher notes depend on the skill of the musician. For voices the normal compass is about two octaves but this may be extended by training.

**composition** The putting together of notes in a certain way which creates an original work of music.

**compound time** This is any musical metre which cannot be classified as *simple time* (where the beat-unit divides into two).

**comprimario** A male singer with a supporting role in Italian opera.

**con** The Italian for 'with', it is often seen in musical instructions such as *con amore* or 'lovingly', *con anima* or 'spiritedly', *con brio* or 'with fire'.

**con spirito** An Italian instruction meaning to play 'in a lively manner'.

**concert master** American title for the first violinist in an orchestra who is usually referred to in Britain as the *leader*.

**concert overture** An instrumental piece of music which opens a concert programme.

**concert pitch** The standard of pitch to which instruments are normally tuned for performance.

**concertante** This means following the form of a concerto using contrasting instruments.

**concertato** Italian for 'roused up' or 'stirred'.

**concertina** An instrument with bellows rather like an accordion but with hexagonal ends and a relatively small number of notes which are sounded by pressing studs.

**concertino** Either a shorter, lighter version of the concerto (see below) or a small group of highly skilled instrumentalists whose playing contrasts with the main orchestra in the *concerto grosso* (see below).

**concerto** The modern use of the term describes a composition, usually in three movements, for one or more solo players and a larger group of musicians. Earlier it referred simply to an orchestral work in several movements, with or without soloists.

**concerto grosso** Italian for 'great concerto', it usually refers to 17th- and 18th-century orchestral works where there is an interplay between the larger group of performers, known as the *'ripieno'* and the solo group or *'concertino'* (see above).

**concord** A chord – a combination of notes played together, which seems complete in itself.

**concrete music** The organization of pre-recorded sounds from nature or the man-made environment.

**conductor** The person who directs a musical performance either with the hands or a baton to ensure that musicians enter at the right time and play together as a group. The conductor is also responsible for the interpretation, determining the changes of tempo, the balance of sound and the nuances of feeling.

**consecutive intervals** The progression of identical intervals in a composition.

**conservatory** *Conservatoire* in French, this is the name of a school for musicians.

**console** The organ desk which contains those parts of the instrument under the organist's control such as the stops, manuals, pedals and pistons.

**consonance** The sounding of two or more notes together to produce a *concord* (see above).

**consort** An old English word for a group of instruments, and therefore a small instrumental ensemble. A 'whole' consort is when the instruments belong to the same family. A 'broken consort' is when the instruments come from different families such as woodwind and strings.

**continental fingering** This system, now universally adopted, numbers the thumb as 1 and the fingers as 2 to 5 in written instructions as to which fingers should be used for which notes. The now obsolete English fingering numbered the fingers 1 to 4 and indicated the thumb by a + sign.

**continuo** Italian abbreviation for 'basso continuo' and sometimes referred to in English as 'through bass'. It is a type of accompaniment, usually for a keyboard instrument, written in a musical shorthand with figures inserted above or below the bass parts so that players can work out the harmonies. It was particularly prevalent between 1600 and 1750.

**contra** An Italian prefix which can either mean 'against' or 'lower in pitch'. The French and German equivalents are 'contre' and 'Kontra' respectively.

**contrabasso** Italian term for double bass.

**contralto** Difference in the length of the vocal chords and the size of the vocal chambers means that individuals have a different range of voices. The contralto is the lowest of the three different ranges of female voice.

**contrapuntal** Composed according to the rules of counterpoint (see below).

**contredanse** French country dance, often more formal than the English equivalent and especially popular in the 18th century.

**coperto** An Italian term meaning 'covered' used to describe the muted sound when drums are covered by a cloth.

**cor** French for horn but used in the names of several instruments which are not horns such as 'cor anglais' (see below).

**Cor anglais** or English horn is a woodwind instrument belonging to the oboe family.

**cornet** This is a wind instrument made from brass or other metal with three valves. It has a cup-shaped mouthpiece and resembles a trumpet though it is shorter and squatter in appearance. It is used mainly in military and brass bands.

**counterpoint** The simultaneous combination of two or more musical parts or voices, each of which is of significance in itself, and which when performed together make musical sense. One melody is then referred to as the counterpoint of the other.

**countertenor** A male voice higher than the tenor and not unlike the alto, though with greater range.

**country dances** English village dances which became popular at the Elizabethan court. Many have been revived by the folk dance movement of the 20th century.

**couplet** A song in which the same music is repeated for each verse.

**cowbell** An orchestral percussion instrument based on the alpine cow bell. With the clapper removed it is tied to a drum and struck with a drum stick.

**crescendo** Italian for 'growing', it means gradually getting louder.

**cross fingering** Fingering the notes on a woodwind instrument in an unusual order so as to obtain sounds which are hard or impossible to obtain normally.

**cross-relation** See *false relation*.

**crotchet** In the United States, often referred to as a 'quarter note'. It is a note which has a quarter the time value of a semibreve or whole note.

**crumhorn** A hook-shaped wind instrument with a double reed which was current in Europe in the 16th and 17th centuries. Made in different sizes for different ranges, it was revived in the mid-20th century to play early music.

**cuivré** The French for 'brassy', and indicating a rather forced, ringing tone.

**cycle** The name given to a set of musical works, especially songs, which are meant to be performed together as a group and are usually linked musically by a common idea or theme.

**cyclic form** A way of linking individual movements, each complete in themselves, in a larger work through a recurrent mood or theme.

**cymbal** A percussion instrument formed from a round sheet of metal. It is either struck with a stick or clashed against another cymbal.

# D

**da capo** An Italian term which means 'repeat from the beginning', sometimes abbreviated to DC. 'Da capo al fine' means repeat from the beginning to the word 'fine' which means end. 'Da capo al segno' means repeat until you reach the specified sign.

**début** From the French word meaning 'beginning', it is used to describe a performer's first important public appearance.

**declamando** An Italian word meaning 'in a declamatory manner'.

**decrescendo** An Italian word for 'decreasing' it indicates that music should become gradually softer.

**degree** A classification of a note by reference to its position on the *diatonic scale*.

**dehors** The French word for 'outside' it is applied to a passage of music which should stand out prominently.

**delicato** An Italian word meaning 'with a delicate touch'.

**délié** The French for 'untied', it can either mean that notes should be separated from each other, or played in a free way.

**delirante** From the Italian, meaning to play in a frenzied way.

**delizioso** A musical passage played in a sweet and sensual way, usually by strings.

**demi** Half, or half-sized. In music, the term often relates to the strength with which something is played. Hence *demi-voix* – half-voice or very softly sung; *demi-tone* – very soft tone produced by underplaying.

**demisemiquaver** An eighth of a crotchet; thus a bar of common time (four crotchets) might contain 32 demisemiquavers.

**descant** The most common usage of the term is where a well-known melody is accompanied by a second melody, usually sung, as a variant to add interest and colour. This second melody may be improvised, and lies in the treble clef, above the original melody.

**détaché** A method of bowing stringed instruments where there is an audible break in tone between notes instead of a continuous stream of sound. This is not to be confused with *staccato,* where each note played is clipped and shortened from its normal length.

**deutscher Tanz** A South German folk-dance form which was often, usually in 3/4 time, used by composers such as Mozart and Schubert.

**development** The part of a composition, usually the second part, where the original themes of a movement are reworked and expanded, modified and combined in new ways, before the third part, the recapitulation, restates the original themes in full.

**diatonic** The scale of eight notes which go to make up any given major or minor scale between one note and its corresponding octave. This involves six whole-tone steps and two half-tone steps. (A whole-tone equals two semitones, or half-tones.) For example: C Major consists of the notes C, D, E, F, G, A, B, C. The two half-tones fall between E to F, and B and C.

**diminished** A term used to describe the size or length of the *interval,* or gap in pitch, between two tones. If an interval is diminished, the gap has been lessened by a semitone, for example from A to A flat. In practice, this term is used only to describe the lessening of the interval of a perfect

fifth, or a minor seventh (see below). A diminished fifth is one semitone lower than a perfect fifth, that is, an interval where the secondary note is the fifth tone above the first note in any given scale. Hence, the perfect fifth of C in the scale of C major is C-G. The diminished fifth is G-flat.

**diminished seventh** The same principle applies to this interval, except that the diminished seventh is made in practice from a minor scale only. The minor seventh is lowered by a semitone, making it, in sound, the same interval as a major sixth. It is the other notes within the given chord which determine whether it is a diminished seventh or not. For example: the notes in a C diminished seventh chord are – C, E flat, G flat, A, whereas the notes in a C major sixth chord are – C, E, G, A. Here, the E flat (the minor third) and G flat (the minor fifth) indicate the minor key which makes the A a diminished seventh; correspondingly, the E (the major third) and G (the major fifth) indicate the major key which makes the A the sixth interval in that scale.

**diminuendo** A gradual reduction of volume in the music. A common abbreviation is *dim.*

**diminution** A way of playing a melody where the time-value for each note is shortened, usually halved, compared to the original.

**dirge** A very slow lament associated with funeral or memorial music.

**discord** The opposite of a concord (see page 103). A chord of two or more notes which sounds incomplete and requires a further chord to achieve resolution.

**dissonance** The sounding of two or more notes together to produce a discord.

**divertimento** A piece, usually for small orchestra, which includes several short, light-hearted movements, not fundamentally connected by any unifying idea. Mozart was especially attracted to this form and composed many such pieces.

**divertissement** Similar in meaning to divertimento. These pieces often accompanied dances, and the musical themes were usually extracted from popular songs or opera arias.

**dodecaphony** A harmonic system which employs the 12-tone principle of 'serial' composition. This was devised by Arnold Schoenberg in 1923, and replaced in his music the traditional major-minor keys. The basic principle gave all 12 tones chromatically available between the octave equal status, as opposed to the importance of the third and the fifth in traditional harmony. The system has been applied with varying degrees of strictness by most of the major composers of this century at one time or another. A chosen note-row becomes the 'tonal reservoir', in all its many combinations, for the work.

**dolce** A direction for the musician or singer to perform a passage in a sweet and gentle manner.

**dolente** To be played in a sorrowful, mournful way.

**dominant** The fifth note of the diatonic scale. This applies to both major and minor keys. For example, the dominant note in the key of C is G.

**doppio** Literally, double. An example of this is *doppio movimento,* which means double the speed of the preceding passage.

**dot 1** In musical notation a dot placed after a note indicates that it is to be extended in time-value by half. **2** A dot placed above a note indicates that it is to be played in a *staccato* (abrupt) manner.

**double bar** A pair of vertical lines close together at the end of a bar to show that a piece of music or a major division in it has come to an end. These lines are often preceded by repeat-marks: two small dots placed, one above the other, in the middle of the stave.

**double bass** The largest and lowest of the violin family of instruments. In orchestras it is most commonly bowed. Also used extensively in jazz and dance music, usually plucked, to stage a constant beat.

**double flat** A sign placed before a note to reduce its given pitch by a whole tone, that is, two flats.

**double sharp** The reverse of the double flat, it raises a given note by a whole tone.

**double stop** The holding-down of two strings simultaneously on a stringed instrument to produce a chord.

**double tongueing** A method of fast note production on brass instruments, especially in long, rhythmically even runs.

**double whole note** See *breve.*

**doucement** Sweetly.

**downbeat** Refers to the stressed beats in a bar – in common or 4/4 time, the first and third beats – which are indicated to an orchestra by the conductor moving his baton downwards. Consequently, the upbeats are the unstressed second and fourth beats in the bar.

**dramatic** Used as a description of voices – soprano, tenor, bass and so on – which have the power and flair to sing successfully forceful operatic roles.

**drone** The parts of an instrument, often of folk-music descent, which produce continuous accompanying notes to the melody. Apart from the bagpipes, this is usually in the stringed instrument family, and indeed Classical Indian music has made a great feature of it. The term is also used to describe music which never deviates from its single bass note.

**drum roll** A fast, continuous pattern of stick-beats on a drum where the beats give the illusion of blurring into a single sustained sound.

**duet** A work, or part or a work, which calls for two voices or instruments to perform together on an equal basis, though for practical purposes one of the two will often take a harmonically subsidiary role.

**dulcimer** An instrument with strings stretched over a soundboard and which are struck by hammers. It became increasingly popular in Europe from the 18th century. Due to the rising popularity of the piano it slowly fell into disuse, and only the Hungarian Cimbalom, a close descendant, is still played today.

**duo** This usually refers to two people who team up to play duets together, especially of the sonata type – for example, violin and piano, two pianos (or one piano four-handed), or violin and cello.

**duple-time** Musical time where the primary metric division is two beats to the bar, or multiples of two, as in 2/4 and 4/4 time.

**duplet** A pair of notes with equal time value occupying the time of three beats. One of the notes may be replaced by a rest.

**Dur** German equivalent of the English 'major' key identification. For example, G Major = G-Dur.

**Durchkomponiert** A literal translation is: 'through-composed'. It is a term used to describe works, especially songs, which are composed in a continuous form of developing parts, none of which is repeated in successive verses. Thus a song in this style is opposite to the *strophic* – form song, where there is deliberate musical repetition.

**dynamics** The degrees of loudness and softness in music.

# E

**écossaise** A type of country dance which was popular in the classical world in Beethoven and Schubert's day. Despite the name, which is French for 'Scottish', the dance has no traceable Scottish ancestry.

**electronic** A type of music using electronic devices in the production of sound. The composing of electronic music was generally an innovation of the post-war years, and differed originally from *musique concrete* in that the sounds were generated exclusively from electronic oscillators.

**elegy** A slow lament, especially for a dead person or an idyllic former time which is now inescapably lost. In classical music the title has come to be applied to both vocal and strictly instrumental music.

**embouchure** The position of the lips, and the muscular displacement to hold that position, used on a wind instrument.

**enchainez** A direction indicating that two sections of a piece should be linked together and played without a break.

**encore** There are two types of encore: 1. The call from an audience (esp. in English) for more playing from the performer. 2. The piece of music the performer responding to this call will play to his appreciative audience.

**English horn** In the US, the name for a double-reeded instrument which is pitched a fifth below the oboe (known in Britain, strangely, as the *cor anglais*). Used principally in orchestral music.

**enharmonic** The description of the theoretical and notative interval between G sharp and A flat, or any other such combination. There is no difference in actual pitch, apart from a fractional variance in instruments such as the voice or violin which are not fixed in pitch.

**ensemble** There is a number of meanings: 1. A group of players or singers who regularly perform together. Usually not particularly large. 2. An operatic piece in which two or more singers are singing simultaneously. 3. The quality of a group of players' teamwork (e.g. 'good ensemble' and 'bad ensemble').

**entr'acte** In French, 'inter-act' – instrumental music played during an intermission or, more rarely, the intermission itself.

**episode** A section of a piece of music which is considered to have a subordinate role. In a rondo, it is a contrasting section between recurrences of the main theme, and in a fugue, it is a section which occurs between entries of the subject.

**equal voices** Voices of the same range: hence, a piece written for 'equal voices' requires multiples of the same voice, e.g. two sopranos, three tenors, and so on.

**equale** A piece of music written for voices or instruments of equal pitch.

**ernst** Serious (from the German).

**estinto** Indicating that a passage should be played with extreme softness, almost without any tone or body to the sound.

**étouffez** A marking which directs the player to immediately dampen or deaden the instrument's tone after it has first been made to resonate. This applies principally to drums and cymbals.

**etwas** means 'somewhat': from the German, e.g. 'etwas langsam', which means 'somewhat slowly'.

**euphonium** A brass instrument pitched in B-flat, used mainly in brass bands. Its range corresponds to the tenor tuba.

**eurythmics** A system of teaching music by emphasizing its rhythmic aspects and the students' response to these rhythms. It has proved to be of great value in general physical and mental education as well as in its specifically musical applications.

**exercise** 1. A piece generally regarded as having no artistic content, written to improve a player's technique. 2. A composition submitted by a student for certain music degrees. 3. An 18th-century short keyboard suite.

**exposition** The part of a composition where the original musical subjects and motifs are first played, before there is any development or elaboration of the basic material.

**extemporize** To freely and spontaneously create themes and musical ideas from any musical basis. It is equivalent to improvisation.

**extravaganza** An exceptionally fanciful composition, or type of stage entertainment with music, especially popular in 19th-century England.

# F

**fa** The name for the note F in Latin countries.

**facile** Easy, fluent. From the Italian 'facilità': ease.

**fado** A 19th-century Portugese folk and popular song. Originating in Lisbon, its particular rhythm and form quickly spread through the countryside as well.

**fagotto** Italian for the bassoon.

**false relation** An English term for the American expression 'cross-relation'. It is a harmonic device where, for example, the notes B and B-flat occur either simultaneously or in immediate succession in different voice or instrumental parts. This creates the situation where the music is not unanimous as to whether the note is to be played or treated as a natural, flat or sharp. When false relations occur they are usually due to the conflict between two essentially melodic parts rather than any real harmonic theory.

**falsetto** Production of a singing voice which is in a register higher than a man's normal singing range. It is the standard method of voice production for the male counter-tenor voice.

**family** This term applies to a set of instruments with common characteristics, such as the violin family (the violin, viola, cello and double bass), or the saxophone family (soprano, alto, tenor, baritone and bass saxophones). The term can also be used to signify a more general grouping, such as 'woodwind', or 'percussion' families.

**fancy** A term used in England in the 16th and 17th centuries for a contrapuntal piece of music, often in several sections, either for a single player or a group of players. Later, the term became absorbed into the wider meaning of the word 'fantasy'.

**fandango** A heavily rhythmic and exciting Spanish dance in triple time, accompanied by castanets and guitar. Often adopted and used by late 19th- and 20th-century composers such as Rimsky-Korsakov and de Falla.

**fanfare** A flourish for trumpets (or occasionally other brass instruments) usually intended as a proclamation or announcing music during a ceremonial or ritual occasion.

**fantasia** A freely-composed instrumental piece where one musical idea flows from another with little regard for the overall form. The impression thus given is one of complete spontaneity.

**fantasy** There are several meanings, all revolving around the relatively free play of ideas which a composer might utilize in a piece of this type: 1. A mood-piece of the Romantic school of the 19th century. 2. A piece built up from a collection of known tunes and melodies.

**farandole** A Provençal dance in 6/8 time. A very ancient form, it has occasionally been utilized by classical composers, and is still used in Provencale.

**faruca** An exuberant Andalusian dance with roots in gypsy music. It has been used by Manuel de Falla, among others.

**feierlich** (German): a direction calling for a solemn, exalted interpretation.

**feminine** A word used generally to connote a relative weakness, a secondary importance to the subject it is attached to – for example, feminine ending, feminine cadence.

**fermata** Pause; from the Italian for 'stop'.

**fiddle** 1. An early form of bowed string instruments without frets which later evolved into the violin. 2. A colloquial term used to express the lighthearted function of the violin in folk music, particularly in folk dance.

**fifth** An interval in melody or harmony of five notes (counting the bottom and top notes) or seven semitones, in either the major or minor scales. For example, C – G, or A – E. This is termed a perfect fifth. The interval of a diminished fifth has one less semitone than a perfect fifth, while an augmented fifth has one extra semitone.

**figure** A short, easily identifiable musical phrase, especially one which is repeated during the composition.

**figured bass** A particular kind of musical shorthand in music manuscripts or scores where the harmony to be played along with a written-out bass part is indicated by numbers only. These numbers relate to the positions of the bass notes and are thus interpreted by the player to mean a specific harmony.

**fin** End (French).

**finale** 1. The last movement of a work with several movements. 2. An ensemble which ends an act of an opera.

**fine** The end (Italian). The term sometimes occurs also in a musical score prior to the finish with the instruction that the player is to go to the end of the composition, then go back to an earlier point and proceed from there again up to where the 'fine' occurs, at which point the performance actually ends.

**fingering** 1. The technique of using the fingers to play an instrument. 2. The indication on paper of which fingers are to be used for which notes, or which sequence of fingers is to be adapted to execute a particular passage. This applies particularly to piano playing.

**first** A term used in orchestras to designate positions of leadership, for example first violins, first trumpet. In a choir the term does not imply leadership, implying only that the lead part is the higher-pitched of the two parts.

**flam** A double beat on a side drum, which is made up of a short note followed by a long note – there are two types, open flam and closed flam, according to the position of the accented beat.

**flamenco** A type of Spanish song chiefly associated with Andalusia. It is often danced to and the flamenco rhythmic patterns are shared by musician and dancer alike. There are many sub-groups and types named after different districts. The whole form is of gypsy and Moorish descent. A type of forceful guitar playing, which uses different fingering to classical guitar as well as percussive effects, is directly linked to this folk form.

**flat** 1. A term indicating a lowering of pitch by a semitone: for example, A-flat is a semitone lower than A-natural. 2. An expression used to indicate that a voice or instrument is playing below the true pitch by mistake – 'they are playing flat'.

**flat keys** These are keys which have flats in their scale. For example, the key of F has one flat, which is B-flat. This is indicated by the key-signature at the beginning of the piece.

**flatterzuge** German for 'flutter-tongue', a technique used in playing wind instruments.

**flautist** The English term for a flute player: derived from the Italian.

**flauto** Italian term for flute.

**flebile** Plaintive, tearful.

**flexatone** A sophisticated version of the musical saw, it operates on the principle of varying tension on the steel blade to produce different tones. Unlike the musical saw, however, it is shaken to produce sound, not bowed.

**florid** A term to denote a highly ornamented musical passage. In the 17th and 18th centuries, these passages were common in Italian opera, where melodies were often greatly embellished by the performer.

**flourish** 1. A trumpet fanfare. 2. A short florid passage used primarily for decoration.

**flügelhorn** A valve-operated wind instrument of the brass family. It comes in various sizes, and is most often used in brass bands, having a mellower tone than either the trumpet or the cornet. Though used occasionally in symphony orchestras, in the past three decades it has been used extensively by jazz musicians.

**flute** 1. A general name for various types of woodwind instruments without reeds, including those used in folk and primitive music around the world. 2. A specific name for the side-blown woodwind instrument which came into standard use in Europe in the 16th century. In latter times it has become common for orchestras and bands to employ metal rather than wooden flutes with metal keys only. As with other instruments in the woodwind family, there are varying sizes, from the piccolo, which is the highest, down through the concert flute and alto flute to the bass flute.

**flutist** In US, a flute-player.

**forlana** The name of an old Italian popular dance, akin to the French gigue.

**form** The layout of, or element of organization in, a piece of music. There are many specific types of musical form in use in classical music: these are dealt with in individual entries.

**forte** Loud (from the Italian). The abbreviation is f.

**fortissimo** Very loud (Italian). The abbreviation is ff.

**fortepiano** An early Italian name for the piano. It is sometimes used in England to denote the late 18th-century piano as distinct from the modern instrument.

**fourth** A melodic or harmonic interval of four steps in the major or minor scale, counting both the first and last notes.

**fractional tone** An interval which is smaller than a semitone.

**free counterpoint** Counterpoint (i.e. the simultaneous combination of two or more melodies to make musical sense) which is not bound by the discipline of what was called strict counterpoint.

**free fantasia** 1. An improvised introduction or prelude, usually for solo keyboard. 2. A name sometimes used to describe the development section of a movement, for example in sonatas.

**frequency** A measure of the pitch of a note derived from the number of vibrations given off in one second. Since 1939 certain pitches have been fixed at agreed frequencies, to aid in tuning, especially in orchestras.

**fret** A strip of wood, metal or gut running across the fingerboard of a stringed instrument to make the accurate fingering of notes and chords easier. An instrument such as the guitar has a number of these frets the whole length of the fingerboard. Conversely, the violin family has never been given frets.

**fretta** Haste, or hurry.

**frottola** A light-hearted Italian song for several voices, popular in the early 16th century, where the main melody in the top voice is accompanied by two or three lower voices.

**fugato** A style of composition suggestive of the *fugue* (see below).

**fugue** A disciplined type of contrapuntal composition for a given number of parts (or 'voices', as they are commonly called), hence the terms 'three-part fugue', four-part fugue', etc. A fugue involves the entry of each voice in succession; the first voice carries the main theme of (the 'subject') of the fugue; this is 'answered' by the second voice. The third voice then enters with the subject, and so on. There are accepted structural principles behind the composition of a proper fugue, and these relate to the melodic shaping of the parts as well as their harmonic positions in relation to each other. There are different types of fugues, often allowing a great deal of variation in the exposition and development of the piece. More complex types include the double fugue and the accompanied fugue. The master of all fugal form was J. S. Bach.

**full anthem** An anthem in the Church of England, sung by the choir for its entirety, with no provision for soloists.

**full score** In the process of writing down a composition for various instruments and then preparing it for publication, there are generally two stages of musical scores used

– the *short score* and the *full score.* The short score is in some respects a musical version of an artist's sketch for a full painting: the composer writes out all the music but does not assign all the different parts to the various instruments he is using. The full score is where the task is completed and every note has been given to the particular instrument meant to play it. Thus the full score is the one which defines the musical colour and texture.

**fuoco** The Italian for fire. A term often used in scores is *con fuoco* – with fire.

**furiant** A fast Bohemian dance containing differing moods and rhythms. Dvořák often used it in his works.

**fz** A common abbreviation for the term *sforzando,* which is a direction indicating that a note or chord should be strongly emphasized.

# G

**G** Note of the chromatic scale. Also the tonic of the scale of G.

**GP** Abbreviation of the musical direction, *General Pause.*

**galant** An 18th-century style of music characterized by its elegance and clarity rather than its intensity of expression. A noted exponent of the style was C. P. E. Bach, son of the eminent J. S. Bach.

**galanteries** In the classical suite there were often movements whose inclusion for performance was optional and intended to provide light relief. These minuets, *gavottes* and polonaises were called galanteries.

**galliard** A lively dance dating back to the 15th century, usually set in triple time. It is no longer in general use. The French variant of the name is *gaillard.*

**galop** A quick ballroom dance in 2/4 time, very popular in the 19th century. The Strauss family made great use of it in their compositions.

**gamba** Abbreviation of viola da gamba.

**gamelan** An Indonesian instrumental ensemble composed of percussive, wind and stringed instruments. Gamelan music, principally of the Javanese and Balinese variety, has had a considerable influence on Western music since 1900.

**gamme** French for scale.

**gapped scale** Any scale which has intervals between notes of more than a whole tone. An example of this is the pentatonic scale, so-called because it comprises only five tones.

**gavotte** An old dance form of French origin, lively in character. It originated as a folk dance but was soon common at court occasions. Often a constituent part of Baroque suites.

**German flute** An obsolete term for the ordinary side-blown flute, as opposed to the *English flute,* the obsolete term for the recorder.

**Ges** German for G flat.

**gesang** German for song, or singing.

**gigue** French for jig.

**giocoso** From the Italian; a musical direction for merry or lighthearted playing.

**gittern** An obsolete form of the guitar dating from medieval times. It was carved from one single block of wood and had four pairs of strings. It was first superseded by the 5-stringed guitar, then by the 6-stringed guitar.

**giusto** A tempo marking meaning strict, or proper. This is calling attention to the allotted tempo and asking that it be accurately adhered to.

**glass harmonica** A simple instrument, now obsolete, made up of drinking glasses of various sizes filled with liquid to give different pitches when rubbed with a damp finger. Mozart once wrote a piece for glass harmonica.

**glee** A short unaccompanied vocal composition in several sections, properly for male voices only. Very popular in Europe for about a century between the mid-1700s and the mid-1800s, it survives to some extent in America. The term glee-club derives from this.

**glissando** A way of playing where a scale is executed in a sliding fashion, quickly and uninterruptedly.

**glockenspiel** A percussion instrument made of tuned metal bars, laid out in the same manner as piano keys, and played with small hammers or mallets, usually hand-held. It gives out a very small, bell-like sound.

**gong** A metal percussion instrument in the shape of a disc, struck with a stick or a hammer. Originally from Asia, the gong became part of Western music in the 19th century. Gongs are usually of indefinite pitch, although some orchestral compositions call for gongs of definite pitch, or at least of differing indefinite pitch.

**grace note** A note meant to be played as an ornament to the main melody. In scores they are often printed in smaller type.

**graciozo** To be played gracefully.

**grand opera** Although now often used vaguely, the term originally described the large-scale and full-blown form of opera that came into vogue in the early part of the 19th century and was to remain popular with composers and public alike till the end of the century. The term is also loosely used to distinguish opera from opperetta.

**grave** From the Italian; a musical indication for a slow, serious tempo.

**Gregorian chant** A form of plainsong which, having its roots in 6th-century religious music, quickly became the standard form in the Catholic Church.

**Gregorian tone** The name of the eight basic melodies of Gregorian chant used by the Catholic Church for the recitation of the psalms and canticles.

**ground** Also called a 'ground bass'. It is a bass line that is constantly repeated, unchanged, throughout a composition while the upper parts proceed in free style.

**guitar** A plucked stringed instrument, it has six strings and a fretted fingerboard. The modern acoustic guitar has a flat back and front, and a pear-shaped body with symmetrical shoulders as well as a round sound hole. The guitar's immense popularity in this century has seen it utilized in virtually every form of Western music, both in its natural acoustic shape and in various solid-body amplified, electronic and even synthesized formats.

# H

**H** German representation for the note B.

**habanera** A fairly slow dance, originally from Cuba. Later imported to Spain – hence the name, taken from *Habana,* the Spanish for Havana. Later became enormously popular and was used as a basis for many other dances, as well as by composers such as Bizet, Ravel and Gottschalk.

**half-note** The American term for a *minim,* where a *semibreve* is a whole-note.

**hand-horn** A horn without valves and therefore capable of producing only a limited natural range of tones.

**harmonic** Relating to harmony (see below).

**harmonica** A small wind-blown instrument with metal reeds, one to each note, capable of both melodic and harmonic playing. Comes in many sizes.

**harmonics** All the sympathetic frequencies of vibration that go together to make up the aural spectrum of a single note, or any particular grouping of notes.

**harmony** Is the simultaneous playing or sounding of notes in a musically organized way so that the combinations have specific musical relationships. It is quite separate theoretically from melody and counterpoint, although all three disciplines have common properties and areas within a given piece where they are to be applied, and thus have overlapping relationships with each other.

**harpsichord** A keyboard instrument, precursor of the piano, where the strings are plucked as opposed to hammered by the playing mechanism.

**head voice** The highest of the registers for the voice: it gives the singer the feeling that the sound produced is vibrating in his or her head, as against the *chest voice,* where the vibrations emanate from the chest and the pitch is lower.

**helicon** A type of tuba which passes round the player's body. An example of this is the Sousaphone.

**hemidemisemiquaver** A note which has the time value of a half a demisemiquaver.

**heroic tenor** Also called by the German equivalent, *Heldentenor,* this is a tenor voice which has the strength and flexibility throughout a large range required to execute extremely demanding opera parts. Often associated with the operas of Wagner.

**hey(e)** Also called a hay(e); a late 16th-century round dance, of no distinctive form, but with a lively rhythm.

**hoe-down** A lively dance, probably of black American origin, which borrowed the characteristics of many dance-forms, including reels and jigs.

**homage** A composition especially popular in the present century, it is a work dedicated to both the name and style of another composer.

**homophony** A type of musical form where the parts, or voices, do not have either melodic or rhythmic independence: all parts move together, as opposed to *polyphony,* where different melodies are interwoven simultaneously.

**horn** A wind instrument through which sound is produced, not by a reed, but by the vibrations of the player's lips into the mouthpiece. The bore of this instrument is conical, distinguishing it from the trumpet, which has a cylindrical bore. Consequently, the tone is full and round. The earliest horns had no valves and could only produce a severely limited range of notes. It was not until the mid-19th century that the coiled horn with valves was developed sufficiently to take its place in the orchestra. These technical developments occured most notably in France. Hence the name *French horn* for the modern orchestral instrument.

**humoresque** An instrumental composition of a witty and capricious nature. Dvorák, Schumann and Grieg all wrote convincing pieces in this style.

**hymn** A religious song of praise, with words usually specially written for it, pointing out its devotional purpose. The hymn has a long history, dating back to the earliest Christian churches.

# I

**idée fixe** A theme which is repeated during a composition, with or without variation. It has a special importance in Berlioz's work, being one of the central techniques in his *Symphonie Fantastique.*

**idyll** A term, adopted from literature, used to describe a peaceful, pastoral work.

**imitation** A device used in part-writing where one voice repeats, either exactly or recognizably, a figure previously stated by another voice.

**impromptu** A short instrumental piece, popular in the last century, which suggests by its nature that it was the result of improvisation, or was written on the spur of the moment. Chopin was a fine exponent of this form.

**improvisation** Music which is made up of entirely spontaneous ideas: these can either be literally conjured up out of nothing – as in free improvisation – or against a pre-set background of chords and melodies. Many composers, such as Liszt and Chopin, were famed for their

improvisations, but in the present century the pre-eminent exponents are to be found mainly in jazz.

**in modo di** Italian for 'in the manner of.'

**indeterminacy** A type of music which evolved after World War II where composers left certain sections, or elements, of a composition to either the discretion of the performer or to chance.

**instrument, musical** Any device or object (other than the human voice) which is used to produce musical sounds. The most common types of musical instrument fall into the wind, stringed and percussion families.

**instrumentation** The task of writing music for particular instruments. This requires knowledge on the part of the composer of the range and types of sound the various instruments possess.

**interlude** A short piece of music played between two other pieces, and sometimes between two acts of a play.

**intermezzo** Taken from the Italian, and meaning 'in the middle'. It refers most frequently to an instrumental piece played in the middle of an opera. Subsidiary meanings include a short piano or chamber work such as written by Brahms and Schumann, and a comic interlude between scenes in an 18th-century opera.

**interval** The distance in pitch between two notes when one is either higher or lower than the other. In Western music this is calculated by counting up the scale from the lower note to the higher. When this is done, both the notes are included in the count: thus the interval from C to A above it is a Sixth, as there is a count of six between the two. The names of intervals are modified according to the harmonic structure surrounding the notes, giving rise to such intervals as Perfect, Major, Minor, Augmented and Diminished thirds, fifths, sixths, etc., as and where appropriate. Where the distance between two notes is more than an octave (eight notes), it is called a *compound interval.* In this case, the upward count is continued until the higher note is reached. For example, the second G after a given C is twelve notes away, and is therefore called a twelfth.

**intonation** Generally used to describe the extent to which a single player or singer, or a group, are in or out of tune. As such, they have either good or bad intonation.

**inversion** The process of turning upside down, and, as it applies to musical harmony, the process of changing the relative positions of the notes in a chord.

# J

**jew's harp** A primitive instrument consisting of a strip of metal held in the mouth and set vibrating by the finger. Different notes are sounded by altering the shape of the mouth cavity. The origin of

the name may be in the spoken corruption of 'jaw's harp'.

**jig** A popular English dance of the 16th century, usually in 6/8 or 12/8 time. It was widely used by theatrical and musical entertainers up to the beginning of the present century, and often made appearance in 18th-century musical suites.

# K

**Kapelle** Originally the German for chapel. It later came to mean the musical staff of a prince's private chapel, and later broadened in meaning to include any orchestra or musical institution.

**Kapellmeister** German for chapel master: originally, the musician in charge of the court chapel. Later it became applicable to the resident conductor, or director, of any instrumental ensemble.

**keen** An Irish funeral song, accompanied by weeping and wailing. Its origins lie in folk-song.

**kettledrum** A drum with origins in the Orient. It has a cauldron-shaped body, and has a single membrane stretched over its top. Kettledrums are tuned to a definite pitch by means of handles around the rim or by a pedal which tightens or slackens the membrane as required.

**key** There are two basic meanings: **1** A lever on a musical instrument, for example a piano or a saxophone, which is depressed to produce a particular musical tone. **2** A scale which is classified by the most important note, known as the keynote. Hence, if the keynote is G, the scale will be either G major of G minor. Compositions are often described as being in a certain key, where its particular scale will predominate for the piece's duration.

**key signature** An indication given in written music to denote the prevailing key of the work being performed. This indication takes the form of sharps or flats entered onto the stave in appropriate places. The key of G, for example would take F sharp.

**keyboard** A continuous arrangement of levers, either for the fingers, as found on the piano or harpsichord, or for the feet, such as the pedal keyboard of an organ.

**klavier** German for keyboard – usually indicating, in modern usage, the piano. Also spelt clavier.

**klavierauszug** German for the reduction of an orchestral or multi-instrumental score to solo piano arrangement.

**klein** From the German – small, or little.

**kornett** The German for Cornet.

**koto** A traditional Japanese instrument, a relation of the zither. It is played on the floor, using three plectrums on the right-hand fingers and thumb, the left hand being used to determine the required tuning by means of a movable bridge. In modern *zokuso,* or koto, compositions, the left hand plucks the strings.

# L

**lament** A piece of music, usually with song, played on sorrowful occasions and signifying deep grief – it is often associated with funerals, or the commemoration of a death.

**lancers** A square dance or quadrille for eight or sixteen couples. It was very popular in the latter half of the 19th century.

**ländler** A slow Austrian dance, in waltz time. It originated in the country, only transferring to the towns after a considerable period. It became fashionable in society during Mozart's and Beethoven's lifetimes. Derives from a German nickname for Upper Austria.

**largamente** Derived from the Italian, largo (slowly), but meant to indicate a dignified and delicate style of playing, or a stateliness of approach.

**larghetto** From the Italian; a direction for a tempo not quite as slow as a largo.

**largo** Literally, 'broad', but taken to mean slow. A basic tempo direction.

**lauda** a vernacular hymn of praise, sung by the *laudisti* community up till this century, originating 600 years ago in Italy.

**lavolta** A leaping dance, popular in Elizabethan times, which involved sweeping the woman partner high into the air. Usually set in fast triple time and syncopated. This dance pattern was occasionally used by Elizabethan composers.

**lay** A form of poetry and music evolved by the French in the 13th century where the irregular stanzas of poetry were set to a varying number of musical phrases which might then be repeated.

**leader** As applied to an orchestra, the leader is the principal first violinist. In the USA and Germany the leader is called the *concertmaster* (Ger., Konzertmeister). He has the responsibility of executing the conductor's wishes in terms of interpretation and expression, leading the rest of the orchestra in such matters. In a chamber group or small ensemble, the leader is the directing member, often again the first violin, where violins are present.

**leading note** The seventh note of the major scale, so-called because it seems to 'lead' to the tonic.

**ledger (leger) line** A short line written above or below the five principal lines of the staff in music scores to accommodate notes which lie outside the compass of the staff.

**legato** From the Italian 'bound together' or 'tied' – a direction to the player that the musical passage is to be played smoothly, so that the notes run into each other.

**leicht** German for light or easy.

**leitmotiv** A musical theme used to identify a character, a subject or a concept in opera. Associated with the operas of Wagner, although also used by earlier composers.

**lento** Slow.

**lesson** A term used in the 17th and 18th centuries for a short piece of music for the harpsichord or organ. Earlier usage covered a variety of instrumental music.

**libretto** Italian for booklet – the text of an opera, or oratorio. Originally printed as a small book for the use of the audience. Usually written by a dramatist or author; less often, by the composer himself.

**licenza** Licence, or freedom – a direction used to indicate some degree of freedom to the performer in question of tempo and interpretation of the relevant passages.

**lieblich** From the German meaning lovely.

**lied** Originally a melodic German folksong, it came to mean all types of solo song with a variety of possible accompaniments. The plural, *lieder,* is nowadays exclusively associated with the German art-song, such as those by Schubert, Schumann and Brahms.

**liedertafel** A male voice choir in German or German-speaking communities. The term, which in translation means 'song table', originates from drinking-gatherings.

**ligature** A band used to secure the reed to the mouthpiece in instruments such as the saxophone and clarinet. Also a slur-mark in vocal music indicating that two or more notes are to be sung to the same syllable.

**litany** An extended form of prayer in the Christian Church, with a series of suppliant verses answered each time by a fixed, unvariant response.

**loco** A direction indicating that the notes referred to should be performed at the written pitch, rather than an octave higher or lower as instructed previously.

**lustig** German for cheerful, merry. To be played in a boisterous way.

**lute** An ancient stringed instrument with a fretted fingerboard and a pear-shaped body. The average lute has six sets (or 'courses') of double-strings, each pair used either in unison or in octave. The instrument is plucked by the fingers.

**lyre** An ancient stringed instrument of very different construction from the lute. It consists of a soundbox with two projecting arms. These support a crossbar from which the strings are stretched down to the soundbox. The lyre can be traced back to Ancient Greece, Egypt and beyond, and it seems to have been used as an accompaniment to singing. The Greeks used a plectrum to pluck the strings; other cultures used the fingers. It is still in use in various forms of ethnic music.

**lyric 1** Originally, a description of the vocal performance with the lyre. The term quickly became less specific and was used to describe opera and both instrumental and chamber pieces. **2** A short, intimate poem disclosing or expressing the writer's personal feelings. The term has been carried over from poetry to music to describe small-scale works such as Grieg's *Lyric Piece.* **3** The words of a popular song. **4** A type of voice; for example, lyric soprano, suggesting a flexible and warm toned voice of expression and nuance.

# M

**Ma., Maj.** Abbreviation of major, often used to save space in catalogues, listings and concert programmes.

**Mi., Min.** Abbreviation of minor.

**MS., MSS.** Abbreviation of manuscript(s).

**madrigal 1** A piece of vocal music which first came to prominence in 14th-century Italy as a form with two or three voice parts. **2** The term was revived in 16th-century England and Italy after its original use had been abandoned. Often written for poetry of the highest quality, these madrigals had three or four voice parts and were contrapuntal in nature. The form was continually added to and developed by a number of gifted composers, reaching a peak in the works of people such as Monteverdi and Marenzio in Italy and Byrd and Morley in England.

**maestoso** An Italian word meaning majestic or dignified.

**maestro** From the Italian for master, a term generally used as a title for conductors and composers, although often used extremely loosely. In Italy, only recognized composers and conductors are accorded the title; in the United States the term is applied to conductors only.

**maggiore** Italian for major (key).

**Magnificat** The canticle, or hymn, of the Virgin Mary, as given in St Luke 1:46–55, and sung at Vespers in Roman Catholic services or at Evensong in the Church of England. Many composers, from Dufay to Vaughan Williams, have set the Magnificat to music.

**major scale** A major scale is made up of a particular order of notes between a given note and its octave. The process is identical for each succeeding octave. A scale is made up of eight notes; for example, to get from one C to the next, there must be six steps of a whole tone and two steps (or intervals) of a semitone. It is the placement of these two semitone stops, between the third and fourth interval, and the seventh and eighth interval, which gives the major scale its distinctive sound. A major key is based on the scale of the same name.

**malguena** A generic name for any of three types of Spanish dance from Malaga or Murcia. Includes singing.

**mandola** A small lute-like stringed instrument with a rounded back and a varying amount of strings, according to the period. Forerunner of the mandolin.

**mandolin** A small instrument which evolved in the 18th century. It has four pairs of strings, tuned the same as a violin and plucked with a plectrum. Although associated with Italian folk music, it has also been used by composers such as Mozart and Mahler.

**manual** A keyboard played with the hands, as opposed to a pedal-board or pedal key-board. Applies mainly to the organ and harpsichord.

**maracas** A rhythm or percussion instrument used in Latin American music. Maracas are composed of bead- or seed-filled gourds placed on sticks. When shaken the gourds give off a dry, crackling sound.

**marcato** A direction for a note or line of notes to be played in a 'marked' or 'emphatic' manner.

**march** A piece of music written expressly for marching soldiers, or military bands. It is usually distinguished by a strong two-step rhythm at moderate or fast tempo, or even 4/4 rhythm at very slow tempo.

**marche** March (French).

**marcia** March (Italian).

**marimba** A type of xylophone greatly favoured in Latin America, but with a history that traces back to an African origin. It is made of wooden resonators tuned in the tempered scale and laid out like a piano keyboard. The tone is more earthy and resonant than the xylophone or its relation, the vibraphone. The bass marimba is also popular throughout the Americas.

**martelé** Hammered. A direction for performance where, in the case of the piano, the notes are sharply accentuated and separated from each other by pressure to the individual keys before and after sounding the tone. With bowed instruments, the bow remains on the strings to control the starting and stopping of the sound.

**marziale** Martial (Italian).

**masque** A courtly stage entertainment popular in 17th-century England. The dance, acting and vocal and instrumental music were all included in one masque to illustrate to the audience predominantly mythological subjects and stories. The masque form is of Italian origin.

**Mass** The Mass is the principal service of the Roman Catholic Church, commemorating the Last Supper, Christ's death and his resurrection. High Mass is sung, Low Mass is spoken. There are two categories of High Mass – the Ordinary and the Proper. The Ordinary was originally set to plainsong but gradually became polyphonic and thereafter more sophisticated as composers set the texts down through the centuries. The Proper deviated from plainsong setting with the relatively recent advent of the Requiem Mass, which composers such as Mozart, Verdi and Berlioz have utilized.

**mattinata** A morning song, or a piece of morning music. Of Italian origin.

**mazurka** A Polish country dance, coming to prominence in the 17th century. It is in triple time, has intricate accents, and can be executed at any speed. Chopin brought the dance to concert music with his 55 mazurkas.

**measure 1** US equivalent for the word *bar* in the metrical division of music. **2** A poetical name for a dance or a dance tune.

**mediant** Counting upwards from the tonic, the mediant is the third note of the scale, in both major and minor scales. For example, B is the mediant of the G major scale.

**melisma** A group of notes in plainsong which are sung to a single syllable. Occasionally, the word *melismatic* is also used to describe any florid lyrical or melodic pattern sung or played over sustained chords.

**mellophone** A simplified version of the orchestral horn; also called a tenor horn. It is often used in marching bands as a substitute for the cornet.

**melodie** French for **1** melody; **2** song.

**melodrama** A dramatic work which has a musical setting or background, but where the dialogue is spoken – this can be for the duration of the work or for particular scenes. Many operas have melodramatic scenes of this type.

**melodramma** Italian meaning opera. Not to be confused with melodrama.

**melody** A succession of notes which vary in pitch and have a recognizable musical shape.

**membranophone** A musical instrument in which sound is produced by striking or rubbing a stretched membrane or skin. For example, all types of drums.

**menuet** French word for minuet.

**menuett** German word for minuet.

**messa** Italian for mass; eg. *messa per i de funti* (mass for the dead, or requiem mass).

**messa di voce** The technique of steady swelling and decreasing in the vocal power of one long-held note.

**messe** French and German for mass; for example *messe des morts, Totenmesse* – mass for the dead.

**mesto** Italian for sad or mournful.

**metà** Italian for half.

**metamorphosis** The process of transformation as applied to musical compositions: chiefly in the way a composer will change and alter a theme many times in the course of a work. Rhythm, tempo, harmony and even some of the theme's notes may be changed, but its essential character remains intact.

**metre** A term borrowed from poetry, where it describes the rhythmic relationship of the syllables in the line of a verse or the lines of a stanza: this was transferred, in music, to the beats in a bar and the bars in a musical phrase.

**metronome** A mechanical apparatus which can be adjusted to sound beats at different fixed rates of speed with constant accuracy when the specific tempo has been selected. Used when practising.

**mezzo, mezza** Italian for half: hence mezzo-soprano (a female voice halfway between true soprano and contralto in pitch); mezza voce (at half-voice, half-power).

**microtone** An interval smaller than a semi-tone. Microtonal intervals have long been used in a wide range of folk and ethnic music, from Eastern Europe to Africa, India and beyond. It is sometimes called a fractional tone.

**middle C** The note C situated approximately at the centre of the piano keyboard. It is tuned to a frequency of 261.6 hertz.

**miniature score** A full printed orchestral score of a musical composition, but reduced in size so as to make it suitable for use by a member of the audience, or for study by a student at home. Normally, only conductors have full scores to follow during a performance; (the rest of the orchestra have just their own parts).

**minim** (In the USA, a *half-note*.) A note with the value of two crotchets, or half a semibreve. Notated by an open circle with a tail. Two minims make up one bar of 4/4 time.

**minstrel** A term used to describe a professional musical performer, from medieval times up to the end of the 17th century; more specifically, the court and social instrumentalists of 14th- and 15th-century France.

**minuet** A French dance in triple time, of rustic or country origin, which became enormously popular in the 17th and 18th centuries. In Baroque music it became the standard third movement of the sonata form, as well as being employed (sometimes twice in one piece) in looser forms such as the serenades and cassation. It was usually flanked by a trio, in triple time, thus creating the basic ABA form of a movement.

**mirliton** An instrument, such as the kazoo, or the paper comb, which uses a vibrating membrane to distort the sounds made by singing or humming against it.

**mirror writing** A strict form of musical inversion where an extended passage – for example, a canon or fugue – is inverted in its entirety, thus creating on paper its exact mirror image.

**miserere** The Roman Catholic name for Psalm 51, which has often been set to music by composers through the centuries.

**missa** Mass. There are various types of Mass which have commonly been set by composers: *missa solemnis* – a full, exalted setting with elaborate music, for example Beethoven's Mass by that name; *missa brevis* – a very concise musical setting of the Mass, such as those composed by Vivaldi and Britten; *missa sine nomine* – a Mass without a name – composed of entirely original material, not based on plainsong or a secular tune; and *missa pro defunctis* – a Requiem Mass, or mass for the dead. Many settings have been made.

**misura** Measure; that is, time measurement in general, or, as it applies to an individual bar.

**mixed voices** A choir made up of both male and female voices; also mixed chorus.

**moderato** Italian for at a moderate pace. Also used in conjunction with other tempo directions such as *allegro moderato* – at a moderately lively speed.

**modes** Forms of scales which were originally used by the ancient Greeks, and later adopted and slightly expanded by medieval musicians, especially in ecclesiastical music. The modes use only the 'white-note' scale on the piano, and consist of different octave (eight-note) segments, for example from C to C octave, or F to F octave. There are seven possible modes in all (i.e. manners of obtaining tonal variety), and each has its own name. For example, there are the *Dorian* and *Lydian* modes. Their usage was generally abandoned in Western music by 1600, when they were replaced by the major-minor organizaton of harmony.

**modo** Manner: *in modo di* – in the manner of.

**modulation** A change of key during the course of a composition, following the rules of natural harmony and the structure of the piece at hand.

**moll** German for Minor (key) – for example, G Moll (G Minor).

**molto** Italian – much, or very: this is used principally in tempo instructions such as molto allegro (very fast).

**monochord** An instrument with a single string and a movable bridge, suspended over a soundbox. It has been in use since ancient Egyptian times.

**monodrama** A stage piece with orchestra, and a relation of melodrama, where the words are spoken rather than sung, but only one character speaks rather than many.

**monody** A word used to describe the single voice-and-continuo type of composition which evolved around the end of the 16th century in direct contrast to the then prevalent polyphonic styles.

**monophony** A composition having a single line of melody, with no harmonic accompaniment.

**monothematic** A composition which has only a single theme. This may apply to a work that has only one movement, or a larger composition which has several movements.

**morbido** Soft, gentle or delicate – this direction is not related to 'morbid'. Hence also morbidessa – delicacy.

**morceau** French, meaning a piece: hence the expression *morceau symphonique.*

**morendo** Dying – a direction indicating that the music should die away and lose force and, sometimes, speed.

**mosso** Moving, fast, or animated.

**motet** Originally this was a piece of choral music, usually in Latin, for use in Roman Catholic services much as anthems are used in the Church of England. The form has been in existence since the 13th century, and the term has been applied to many different compositional approaches, right up to such modern composers as Bruckner, Parry and Poulenc.

**motif** French – sometimes used in English for leading motive.

**motion** a term used to describe the progress of a melodic line upwards or downwards in one or more parts. There are a number of different types of motion and terms to describe them: a single

melody moves in either conjunct or disjunct motion (i.e. moving to adjacent notes or by larger steps), while two melodies may move in similar, contrary or oblique motion. These three terms are self-explanatory if you picture the notes on the staff. Parallel motion, finally, preserves the same interval between the two melodies.

**motiv(e)** A short, recognizable melodic or rhythmic figure, several of which may contribute to a theme. The word is often used to indicate the smallest unit capable of sustaining musical analysis.

**moto** Motion; hence con moto – with movement.

**motto** A theme which recurs during the course of a composition, in the manner of a quotation, either transformed or not.

**movement** A self-contained section, or part, of a larger composition, such as a concerto or symphony in orchestral music, or a sonata or string quartet in solo or chamber music.

**movimenti** Speed or motion.

**muffle** To reduce the sound of a drum by covering its surface with a cloth.

**musette 1** A type of bagpipe popular in France in Louis XIV's reign. **2** A musical piece, similar to a gavotte, with a bass drone to suggest the above instrument. **3** An oriental instrument, with a similar sound to an oboe, though with a simpler fingering procedure based on holes and a few keys.

**music drama** A term used by Wagner to describe his operas after *Lohengrin* – the term 'opera' at that time seemed inadequate.

**musical box** A clockwork mechanism which, through the use of rotating pins in a fixed pattern, produces a certain melody. Popular as a toy in the 19th century.

**musical comedy** A type of play with music. Popular at the turn of the present century, it later evolved into 'the musical'.

**musical saw** (singing saw). An ordinary wood saw which, stroked with a violin bow and bent accordingly, produces different tones. Used in barn dances.

**musicology** The academic study of music.

**musique concrète** A name coined in the post World War II period to describe composed or 'organized' music which extensively utilized pre-recorded or pre-existing sounds, often taken from everyday life. These included such things as car noises, footsteps, vacuum cleaners and conversation mixed together to varying degrees with conventional notated music. The movement has now been absorbed into the mainstream of electronic music.

**muta** (pl. mutano). Italian for change: ie. a direction to the musician to change either to a different instrument or tuning.

**mute** A device fitted to an instrument to make it softer or weaker in tone. Mutes come in all shapes and sizes, as appropriate for the instrument to be muted. Mutes are also used in music such as jazz to produce varying controlled distortions of tone.

# N

**nachtanz** After-dance: a fast dance, the second of a pair.

**Nachtmusik** Night-music: a composition intended as a serenade, performed in the evening, originally in the open air.

**natural 1** A note which is neither sharp nor flat. **2** A note designated by the sign ♮ to indicate that it is played as a natural and not as a sharp or flat as designated by the key signature.

**naturale** A direction that the voice or instrument used should return to its usual manner after a passage requiring an unusual technique.

**neck** The part of a stringed instrument which carries the fingerboard.

**neo** From Greek meaning 'new'. Used in classifying musical styles to indicate a revived or newly adapted older style now used in a different context: e.g. Neo-Classical, neo-Romantic. Terms which have been applied to phases of the careers of Stravinsky and Vaughan Williams respectively.

**new music** A term that has been applied at various times in Western music history. **1** Ars Nova of the 14th century. **2** A style pioneered by Caccini in the early 17th century. **3** The music of Liszt and Wagner, as against Brahms. **4** Early 20th century serialism and atonality.

**niente** Italian for nothing. For example – *a niente* (to nothing) or *quasi niente* (almost nothing) indicates level of volume or tone at which to play.

**ninth** An interval of nine steps, counting upwards and including the first and last note in the diatonic scale.

**nocturne** or **notturno** Night-piece. The term describes a short piece of music, related to the serenade, suggestive of calm and reflection. Taken up by composers such as Chopin, Debussy and Britten and applied in different contexts, but still closely connected to the idea of a meditative, pensive atmosphere.

**nonet 1** A composition for nine voices or instruments. **2** A group consisting of nine voices or instruments.

**non-harmonic note** A note which has no harmonic association with the chord it precedes or follows.

**notation** The writing down of music so that it is symbolically recorded for others to perform. Symbols historically associated with Western music are used, as are letters and abbreviated combinations of the two.

**note 1** A single sound of given pitch and fixed duration. **2** The symbolic notation for **1**. **3** A lever or key on an instrument for the production of a particular sound.

**nut 1** The ridge – between the pegs and the fingerboard – on the neck of a stringed instrument over which the strings pass. Thus an open string vibrates between the nut and the bridge. **2** A device fitted to the bow of a violin to enable its tension to be adjusted.

# O

**obbligato 1** Not to be omitted in performance ie. the part written for an instrument or section of the orchestra which must be played. **2** The term used by some composers to imply the opposite – that the part so indicated may be omitted. **3** A corruption of the term in popular 20th-century music to describe an accompanying instrumental interplay behind a principal melody.

**oboe** A double reeded instrument of the woodwind family. Developed in 17th-century France and 18th-century Germany, it evolved into the standard 19th-century modern instrument pitched in B-flat with a complicated set of keys. Three basic types are commonly used – the cor anglais, the oboe d'amore and the regular oboe.

**octave** An interval of eight diatonic steps, counting the top and bottom notes.

**octet 1** A composition for eight voices or instruments. **2** A group composed of eight voices or instruments.

**ode 1** A musical setting of a poem written in ode form. **2** Loosely used to describe a composition set on a specific theme, such as Stravinsky's *Ode: Elegiacal Chant.*

**open form** A composition where the performers are meant to use their discretion as to where to start and end in the score. Karlheinz Stockhausen is a noted exponent of this form

**open harmony** Harmony in which the notes of the chord are separated by large intervals.

**open string** On a stringed instrument, when the string played is unstopped by the fingers. Applies to both plucked and bowed stringed instruments and is often exploited by composers seeking a particularly resonant sound.

**opera** A dramatic composition in which the characters sing rather than speak the text, or at least there is a preponderance of sung text, accompanied by an orchestra. The music is central in binding together the story, the themes and the characterizations. The form arose in Italy around the beginning of the 17th century, and principal early exponents were Peri and Monteverdi. Some claims are made for the inclusion of certain medieval works under this title, though at present the issue is still debated. Since early times opera has developed rapidly and has reflected the changing musical climates of subsequent periods right up to the modern day.

**opéra bouffe** A light, witty and satirical form of opera popular in France in the late 19th century. Derived from the Italian, *opera buffa.*

**opéra comique 1** French term describing a French comic opera with spoken dialogue, generally with heroic or mythological subjects. **2** In the 19th century an opéra comique could be any opera with spoken dialogue, with either serious or comic intent. Gounod and Bizet wrote operas of this type.

**opera seria** This term signified a serious opera, with a heroic or tragic plot, and was the 18th century opposite to opera buffa, although people at the time tended to use the expression *dramma per musica* more often. Rossini is generally regarded as the last composer in this idiom.

**operetta** Literally, operetta means little opera, and was originally a description of the short, light and generally entertaining forms of opera developing from opéra comique in the mid 19th century. It later came to mean a comic or satiric opera of any length, especially French or German, such as written by Offenbach, J. Strauss and Lehar.

**opus** (abbreviation: op. ) From the latin, meaning 'work'. A composer's works are often catalogued so that each individual composition has its own 'opus' number. Works are usually numbered in roughly the same order as they were written. Sometimes, a single opus number may include within it a number of works, as the composer intends the works to be seen as a whole, and not in isolation – for example, 'Opus 5 No. 2'.

**oratorio 1** A work for the stage in more or less dramatic form but intended for the concert hall, not the theatre. It includes solo singers, choruses and an orchestra in its typical form but no action.

**Orchestra** Large group of instrumentalists, usually including a section of bowed instruments of the violin family, a section of wind instruments, subdivided into woodwinds and brass, and a percussion section. The numbers of players and the precise instrumentation vary with each piece of music played, and the orchestra can therefore have a qualifying title such as Chamber Orchestra, Symphony Orchestra, etc.

**orchestration** Scoring a musical piece for an orchestra or a large body of different instruments, or arranging solo music for an ensemble.

**organ** A keyboard instrument in which the principle of sound production is one of air flowing through pipes. The instrument is of great antiquity and has undergone enormous development. A system of different pipes for the same note enables the organ to achieve tonal variations through the use of stops near the keyboard which direct the air current. In the present century these principles have been adapted for the electronic organ, where electronic impulses serve instead of the wind pipes.

**organ mass** A setting of the Mass in which portions of the text are sung in alternation with parts for the organ.

**organistrum** An early form of the hurdy-gurdy.

**orgel, orgue** German and French names for the organ, respectively.

**ornament** An embellishment to the original melody of a piece, either written out by the composer or added by the performer when extemporizing.

**ossia** A term used to indicate an alternative passage in a musical score, often used where the original passage is extremely difficult to execute, and the composer writes out an easier alternative.

**ostinato** A continually repeated melodic and rhythmic figure.

**overblow** To blow a wind instrument with such force that upper harmonic tones (*overtones*) are produced.

**overtones 1** Any note in a harmonic series except the first (called the *fundamental*). **2** The sounds created when the higher frequencies of a vibrating body are dominant.

**overture 1** A piece of orchestral music prefacing an opera, oratorio or play, usually including musical themes from that which is to follow. **2** A one-movement orchestral work, such as Mendelssohn's *Hebrides Overture,* intended for the concert hall and often alluding to a literary subject. These works are properly called concert overtures.

# P

**p** An abbreviation of *piano* (Italian for 'soft'). Additional *ps* indicate successive reductions in volume.

**palindrome 1** A word or sentence which, when reversed, reads exactly the same. **2** A piece of music with the same qualities.

**panpipes** An ancient instrument, consisting of a set of simple flutes of different lengths joined together. Different notes are produced by blowing across the tops of the different pipes.

**pantomime 1** A dumb-show or mimed play, or dramatic entertainment, either self-contained or part of a larger work. It is used in both spoken and musical dramas. Modern pantomime includes songs. **2** A British Christmas-time stage entertainment, traditionally for children and based on a fairy-tale.

**pantonality** A term used to describe an approach to composition adopted by many of this century's composers. It is an approach to tonality where tonal centres intermingle and constantly shift without being established in the traditional manner. Bartók, Stravinsky and Hindermith all used this technique.

**parlando** An indication that the singer should either speak the passage thus marked, as in opera, or that a passage in a song requires something closer to speech.

**part 1** The music written for a particular voice or performer in an ensemble. **2** A strand of melody, whether or not it is performed by one or more, in polyphonic music. **3** A section of a large-scale work, such as an oratorio, roughly corresponding to the acts of an opera, to enable breaks to be taken by both performers and audience.

**partials** The notes of the harmonic series

produced when a string or column of air vibrates. The first partial is the fundamental tone, the upper partials are the various overtones.

**partita 1** A set of variations, each known as a parte, as composed in the 17th and 18th centuries. **2** A suite of pieces.

**passage-work** A passage in a composition that calls for fast and brilliant playing rather than displaying any great import or originality to the piece as a whole.

**passing note** An incidental note in a composition which creates a dissonance with the chord or prevailing harmony but which is justified by its leading into the next chord, where it is usually consonant.

**Passion** A musical setting of the biblical story of Christ's death.

**pasticcio** A composition, most often an opera, created by an amalgamation of music by different composers.

**pastoral 1** Music with a rural theme. **2** Obsolete term used to describe an early type of opera. **3** A melodic piece in flowing 3/4 time, originating in rural Italy.

**patter song** A comic song in which the words are sung as quickly as possible. Often associated with operetta and musicals.

**pausa** Rest (not pause).

**pause** (English) **1** A sign in musical notation meaning that the note so marked must be held longer than its time value would normally indicate; the actual length is usually at the performer's discretion. **2** Used in the phrase 'general pause', meaning a rest of at least one bar for the entire ensemble.

**pause** (German) **1** A pause. **2** A rest. **3** An interval in a concert.

**pavan(e)** A slow, stately court dance originating in the 16th century or even earlier. Normally in two-step time and with simple, repetitive steps. It spread from Padova (Italy) to the rest of Europe, reaching its musical climax in the compositions of the English virginalists.

**pavillon** The bell of a wind instrument.

**pedal 1** In musical harmony, this is a note sustained in the bass under changing harmonies. An inverted pedal is a pedal note not actually in the bass but in a higher register. **2** The lowest note of the harmonic series, especially where it concerns the playing of brass instruments. **3** A lever operated by the feet, especially applied to pianos and other keyboard instruments.

**pedal-board** A keyboard played by the feet.

**pedal-piano** A piano which has a pedal keyboard affixed in addition to its standard keyboard for hands.

**penillion** A traditional type of Welsh singing, to the accompaniment of a harp.

**pentatonic** From the Greek pente (five), used to describe a scale of just five notes, often approximated by the five black keys of the piano. This scale, in various tonalities, is at the basis of much folk music all over the world.

**percussion** A musical instrument family where the sound is created by a resonating surface being struck, usually by a stick or a hand. The term includes instruments which are capable of being tuned to various pitches as well as instruments which give off indefinite pitch.

**perfect 1** A term used in harmony to describe the intervals which are the same in both the major and minor keys – that is, the fourth, fifth, and octave. These intervals, when moved from their basic positions, become either diminished or augmented if lessened or enlarged respectively by a semitone. **2** Used in the phrase 'perfect time' which, in medieval music, means triple time.

**perfect cadence** A type of progression which establishes a key or mode at the end of a phrase, a section or the end of a composition. The perfect cadence moves from the dominant, or dominant seventh, to the tonic, thus conveying a sense of completeness and finality.

**perpetuum mobile** A piece of music in which there is a constant use of rapid and repetitive note values, thus conveying a sense of machine-like speed.

**pesante** Heavy or heavily – a direction indicating that a passage should be played with firm emphasis.

**pezzo** A piece, i.e. a play, or a piece of music, etc.

**philharmonic** Literally, to be fond of music. It does not denote any particular type of orchestra, although the word is often used as part of an orchestra's name.

**phrase** A group of notes which form a section or unit of melody.

**phrase-mark** A line in musical notation which indicates which bars will go to make up a musical phrase.

**piacere, a** Literally, at pleasure, i.e. at the performer's discretion. It applies mainly to the waiving of the necessity to observe strict time.

**piacevole** Agreeably, pleasantly.

**piangendo** Plaintive or weeping.

**pianino** A small-size upright piano.

**pianissimo** Very softly.

**piano 1** Soft, softly. **2** English word for the hammer-action keyboard instrument which first reached wide popularity in the 18th century and eventually replaced the harpsichord. From the 18th-century Italian *gravicembalo col piano e forte* (harpsichord with soft and loud).

**pianoforte** Italian for piano.

**pipe 1** A hollow cylinder or tube used to produce a musical sound or tone through air vibrations, e.g. organ pipes. **2** A type of one-handed whistle flute.

**piston** Valve on a brass instrument, which when depressed, alters the length of the tube and therefore its harmonic series.

**pitch** The property, or quality, according to which a musical note or sound is determined as high or low in contrast to the different notes around it. Pitch is measured and defined through the precise number of vibrations per second needed to create a given sound.

**piu** More: e.g. piu lento: more slowly; piu allegro: more quickly.

**pizzicato** Indicates that a passage should be played by plucking the strings of a bowed string instrument.

**plainsong** The single line of unaccompanied vocal melody in free rhythm to which texts of the Roman Catholic liturgy are sung. Plainsong or plainchant reached a peak in the Middle Ages, when Gregorian chants were the dominant form.

**player piano** Mechanically adapted piano which plays itself through a series of prearranged methods – mostly through the coded instructions of holes punched in a paper or metal roll which is rotated by pedalling.

**plectrum** Small flat piece of plastic, wood, steel or shell which is used to pluck the strings of such instruments as the mandolin, banjo and guitar.

**poco** A little, slightly: e.g. un poco crescendo: a small increase in volume.

**polka** Dance in brisk, vigorous double time. Originally a Bohemian peasant dance, it became immensely popular all over Europe in the mid-19th century. Many composers, notably the two Johann Strausses, wrote polkas.

**polonaise** Stately dance in 3/4 time, originating in Poland, probably in 16th-century courtly celebrations. Bach used the form in his Sixth French suite, but it did not become really popular until the early 19th century by which time it had changed radically. Chopin's 16 highly patriotic polonaises are the most famous compositions in this form.

**polymodal** Music which employs simultaneously the scales of at least two of the old modes at different pitches.

**polyphonic** Music which has two or more parts, each part having an independent melodic line. The use of counterpoint is central to the concept of polyphony. It was the dominant form of music between the 13th and 16th centuries, up to the time of Bach, and this time is sometimes known as the 'polyphonic period'.

**polyrhythmic** Music which employs several separate rhythms or rhythmic patterns simultaneously. Long noted in the ethnic music of many cultures, polyrhythms are an outstanding feature of modern Afro-american music.

**polytonal** Music written in more than one key simultaneously. Both Milhaud and Holst have used polytonality extensively, as did Charles Ives. Music written in two keys only is called 'bitonal'.

**portamento** Literally meaning 'carrying', portamento means gliding without a break from one note to the next when singing or playing a stringed instrument or trombone.

**position** In harmony, the layout of a chord, determined solely by what note is at the bottom of the chord. If the lowest note of the chord is the keynote, the chord is in the 'root' position. Other positions are known as 'inversions', as the lowest note of the chord is taken progressively higher.

**post horn** Brass instrument without valves or keys, and just a single tube, which is either straight or coiled. It is capable of playing only a single harmonic series.

**postlude** The opposite of a prelude, often an organ voluntary at the end of a church service, and equally vague in its application to a piece of music.

**pot-pourri** Used to describe a loosely connected musical medley, often of folk origin, and occasionally with connecting phrases between the melodies.

**praeludium** Latin for prelude.

**prelude** An instrumental piece preceding a larger work, used as an introduction to it; the term has also been used to describe a miniature or a series of miniatures for piano which are essentially self-contained and refer to no other following piece.

**prepared piano** A piano which has had its mechanics, and especially its strings, tampered with so as to produce unusual and unexpected sounds by playing the keyboard conventionally.

**pressez** Increase speed.

**prestissimo** Very fast.

**presto** Fast; i.e. faster than allegro.

**primo, prima** Italian for first: hence, prima donna – chief female singer; tempo primo – same tempo as the first one; Prima volta – first time.

**principal 1** The leader of a section of an orchestra, such as the trumpets, or the flutes, would be the principal trumpet, or principal flute. **2** A singer who takes lead roles in opera.

**programme music** A work which is meant to be an illustration of, or an interpretation of, a non-musical idea.

**progression** Orderly motion from one chord to the next.

**psalm** A setting of one of the 150 songs from the Book of Psalms in the Old Testament.

**psalter** An edition of the Book of Psalms, often with music indicated.

**psaltery** An ancient type of zither, or lyre.

# Q

**quadrille** A type of square dance brought into popularity during Napoleon's reign; enjoyed enormous vogue in 19th century England and became formalized as a dance with five different sections.

**quadruplet** A group of four notes of equal time value played in the space of three notes, five notes or some other number in the time signature.

**quarter-note** US equivalent of the European *crotchet.*

**quarter-tone** An interval between pitches of half a semitone. This interval was not used in Western art-music until the present century, but has been ever-present in a great many of the world's ethnic musics as well as Oriental classical music.

**quartet 1** A performing group composed of four instruments or singers. **2** A piece written for four performers or singers.

**quasi** Almost, or nearly.

**quaver** A note which in time value is half a crotchet, or two semi-quavers.

**quintet 1** A performing group composed of five instruments or singers. **2** A piece written for five performers or singers.

**quodlibet** A piece containing a medley of several popular tunes woven together in an ingenious and unusual way.

# R

**ragtime** A style of music brought to prominence by black and creole US musicians and composers. A precursor to jazz, it is distinguished by its evenly syncopated march-like rhythms and its general avoidance of harmonic patterns based on the blues. Composers such as Debussy, Ravel and Stravinsky all used this form but the greatest was Scott Joplin.

**rallentando** Slowing-down.

**rasch** Quick.

**rattle** A shaken percussive instrument.

**realization** A working-out in full of a composition left incomplete or sparsely notated by its composer.

**recapitulation** The part of a composition in which the original themes and subjects are repeated after they have been developed.

**recitative** A type of melodic speech, in dialogue or narration, used in opera to speed the development of the plot.

**recorder** An end-blown woodwind instrument without a reed which comes in a variety of sizes. It was largely ousted in popularity by the side-blown flute.

**reed instruments** Musical instruments using a cane reed mouthpiece which, when blown, produces the vibrations which give off the sound.

**reel** A fast dance for two or more couples; a national dance of Scotland.

**refrain** A recurring part of a song, usually at the end of each stanza or verse.

**register 1** A set of pipes on an organ controlled by a single stop. **2** Part of the range of the human voice with a distinctive character of its own. **3** The corresponding ranges of musical instruments.

**related keys** Musical keys which are harmonically similar, thus making movement (modulation) between them relatively easy.

**relative** These are major and minor keys which share the same key signatures, for example E-flat major and C minor, or E minor and G major.

**repeat** An instruction in a musical score to perform a section again.

**répétiteur** An opera company member who coaches the singers and plays the piano at rehearsals.

**reprise 1** A repeated part of a work. **2** A restatement of the first subject in a sonata at the beginning of the recapitulation. **3** The reappearance of a melody or song in an operetta, suite or musical.

**requiem 1** A musical setting of the Roman Catholic Mass for the dead. Many hundreds of settings have been made, from the time of plainsong up to the present century. **2** A non-sectarian, even non-religious musical composition in the form of a commemoration of the dead.

**resolution** A progression from discord to concord in harmony.

**rest** An indication in a musical score that there is to be silence, either for the players indicated or for the entire ensemble.

**retrograde** The term used to describe a theme played backwards.

**rhapsody** A word used by composers to describe open-form works in one continuous movement, often incorporating folk forms or other sources of romantic inspiration. The name does not denote any particular musical form.

**rhythm** The placing of notes in a sequence determined by their distribution and accentuation in the passing of time.

**ricercar** A particular form of instrumental piece much in use in the 16th and 17th centuries, contrapuntal in form.

**riff** A continuously repeated musical phrase, often with subtle rhythmic and melodic variations.

**ritardando** Slowing down; a musical direction to a performer.

**ritenuto** Held back; keeping the tempo held back.

**ritmo** Italian for rhythm.

**ritornello** A recurring passage in a work, often used to separate different sections of the piece in question.

**roll** A succession of controlled drumbeats played so fast as to give a virtually continuous percussive sound.

**romance** A wide and vague term, not dissimilar to rhapsody, used to describe music which is essentially melodic and romantic, even sentimental, in character.

**rondeau 1** A type of medieval song prevalent in France. **2** A 17th-century French form using a refrain followed by differing couplets.

**rondo** A type of composition where one section recurs intermittently among differing sections. This loose scheme was favoured by many Baroque and Classical composers.

**root** The lowest note of a chord when it is in its basic position eg. the root of the G major chord in its G-B-D position is G. This chord is thus in root position.

**round** A short type of canon for unaccompanied voices where each voice in turn sings a complete melody at the same pitch, or in the octave.

**rubato** A direction giving the player a degree of freedom when it comes to the time values and rhythm of certain indicated notes and phrases, thus increasing the expressivity of the music, although it is not to imply an abandonment of the pulse or beat.

**rumba** A Cuban dance in 8/8 time with a sinuous pattern of emphasis in the beat.

**R.V.** An abbreviation of Ryom Verzeichnis, used as a prefix for the catalogue numbers assigned to Vivaldi compositions by the musicologist Peter Ryom in 1974.

# S

**sarabande** A slow dignified dance introduced to Europe, through Spain, in the 16th century. The dance probably has a longer history in the East.

**saxhorns** A group of brass wind instruments, seven in all, invented last century by Adolphe Sax, and similar in construction to flügelhorns.

**saxophone** A member of the single-reed brass instrument family invented by Adolphe Sax. It has enjoyed immense popularity in 20th-century popular music, and has been used by many composers, including Milhaud, Debussy, Berg, Stravinsky and Glazunov.

**scale** A progression, or series of steps of single notes, either upwards or downwards.

**scena** A 19th-century concert-work for solo voice and orchestra in several movements.

**scherzando** A direction indicating music played in a playful or lighthearted manner.

**scherzo** A lively movement, usually in 3/4, developed greatly by Haydn, Beethoven and their contemporaries from the minuet and used as a lighter contrast to the surrounding movements.

**schleppend** A German tempo instruction, meaning to drag. Nicht schleppend indicates the opposite.

**schnell** German for fast.

**schottische** A 19th-century ballroom dance in 2/4 time, related to the polka but generally slower.

**scoop** A singing fault where the note is approached from below rather than attacked cleanly and accurately.

**scordatura** Tuning of a stringed instrument to notes other than normal, thus altering the range and colour.

**score** The combined music for all the parts of a vocal or instrumental composition. The conductor usually has the full score while individual players usually read from scores showing only their own parts.

**scorrevole** A tempo and rhythmic direction – to be played in a gliding, rapidly fluent way.

**second 1** An interval of two steps in the major or minor scale, counting the bottom and top notes: two semitones for a major second, one semitone for a minor second. **2** The description of a lower-pitched part in a vocal or instrumental score e.g. second violin, second trumpet, etc.

**segno** Sign: e.g. al segno: play as far as the sign; or dal segno: from the sign – a direction to repeat the preceding passage beginning from the sign.

**segue** A direction to proceed on to the next section without pause.

**semibreve** (In the USA, a *whole-note.*) A note with the time-value of half a breve and twice that of a minim.

**semiquaver** (In the USA, a *sixteenth-note.*) A note with the time-value of half a quaver.

**semitone** This is the smallest commonly used interval in Western art music, and is the interval to be found between any one note and the next on the piano, whether white or black. In the chromatic scale, all the steps are semitones.

**semplice** A direction to perform a piece in a simple manner.

**senza** Without.

**septet 1** A composition for seven voices or instruments. **2** A group composed of seven voices or instruments.

**sequence 1** The repetition of a phrase at a higher or lower pitch. **2** A hymn-like composition set to non-biblical Latin texts, sung during High Mass or a Requiem Mass.

**serenade** Originally a piece of open-air evening music, the term came to be used to describe an assortment of romantic-sounding orchestral works loosely associated with the night.

**serenata 1** Serenade. **2** An 18th-century English word for an operatic cantata.

**serialism** A form of composition in which the pitches are ordered in a 'serial' way. Used extensively this century, the classical example of this technique is Schoenberg's dodecaphony, or twelve-note music.

**series** A set or sequence of notes treated by the composer as raw material from which to order and construct a composition according to the tenets of serialism.

**service** A setting of the Canticles and Responses from the Church of England Book of Common Prayer.

**seventh** An interval of melody or harmony which takes seven steps in the major or minor scales, including the bottom and top notes.

**sextet 1** A composition for six voices or instruments. **2** A group of six voices or instruments.

**sextuplet** A group of six notes, or notes and rests, of equal time value which are played in the space or time of four notes.

**sforzando** A direction that a note or a chord is to be played in a forced, strong manner, or strongly emphasised.

**sharp 1** A sign placed in front of a note to indicate that it is raised by a semitone. **2** An expression used to indicate that an instrument or voice is pitching above the required note in error.

**sharp keys** Keys which have sharps in their key signatures, as against flats.

**sight read** The ability to play an instrument or sing according to the written notes, at first sight.

**simile** Similar; that is, the performance should continue as before.

**simple interval** An interval between two notes of an octave or less. Any interval more than an octave is a compound interval.

**simple time** Any form of metrical time in music where the beat is divisible by two.

**sinfonia** A piece of instrumental music in an early 18th-century opera. It is now occasionally used as a much looser term describing a serious orchestral work.

**sinfonia concertante** An orchestral work, especially around the time of Haydn and Mozart (for example, a double or triple concerto). The term is still occasionally used to denote a concerto with a more than usually integrated score between soloist and orchestra.

**sinfonietta 1** A symphony-like work which is smaller and lighter in intent than a full symphony. **2** A small symphony orchestra.

**sixteenth-note** US term for the British *semi-quaver.*

**sixth** An interval of six notes (counting the first and last notes) between the lower and upper note. For a major sixth, there must be nine semitones, and for a minor sixth, there must be eight.

**sketch 1** A rough draft of a composition. **2** A short, often evocative piece of music, written in an undemanding manner.

**slentando** Slowing down.

**slide 1** The technique on stringed instruments of moving from one note to another with the same finger without removing it from the string. **2** The basic mechanical action of the trombone which enables the full chromatic range to be reached through different positions on the slide, rather than by the use of valves.

**slur** A curved line over two or more notes indicating that they are to be played as one unbroken phrase.

**soave** Italian direction indicating music played sweetly, or gently.

**solmization** A system for designating musical notes by syllables, first adopted as early as the 11th century, on a Latin basis. Modern syllabic equivalents are based on the Italian, paralleled in English by doh, ray, me, fah, soh, lah, te, doh. These notes can represent any eight-note scale.

**solo** A piece, or passage from a piece, performed by a single player or singer.

**sonata** Originally, an instrumental piece of music in no recognized form, as opposed to a vocal piece. Later, it developed out of such multiple-movement forms as the ricercar and canzona into its own three-or-four movement shape, which reached its classic expression with the advent of Haydn and Mozart. By the middle of the 19th century, it was often cast as a single movement, and the form was identified as a work for one or two players.

**sonata-form** A term used to describe the typical structuring of the first movement of a sonata which evolved in the latter part of the 18th century. The form is by no means restricted, however, to first movements, or even to sonatas, and can crop up also in a vocal work, for example.

**sonatina** A short, relatively easy sonata, lighter in expression than a regular sonata: means, literally, 'little sonata'.

**song** A short piece of music for the voice, whether solo or accompanied.

**song-cycle** A group of songs ordered in a sequence for performance, so as to reflect a central idea or theme.

**sopranino** A term for musical instruments pitched higher than soprano range. An example is the sopranino saxophone.

**sostenuto** Sustained: the music is to be played in a smooth, flowing style.

**sotto voce** Literally, 'under the voice': a direction that the music be played in a barely audible, or hushed, manner.

**speech song** From the German *Sprechgesang:* a type of song where the vocal enunciation of the text is halfway between singing and speaking, where a note is suggested but not sustained.

**spinet** A harpsichord-type keyboard instrument, popular between the 16th and 18th centuries, smaller than the harpsichord, and with a basic wing-shape.

**stabat mater** A medieval hymn used in the Roman Catholic Church; the words have been set to music many times by composers right up to the present day.

**staccato** From the Italian meaning detached. A musical direction indicating that the notes so marked should be played in such a manner that they are quite distinct from each other.

**staff (stave)** The framework of lines and spaces between, on which musical notation is written.

**stimme** A German word meaning: **1** a voice; **2** an instrumental part in a composition.

**stop 1** A knob or lever on an organ controlling the use or suspension of the rank of pipes, thus controlling the overall type or volume of sound produced. **2** To stop a string is to place a finger on it; therefore a stopped string is the opposite of an open string, where the string is played without touching the fingerboard.

**stringed instruments** Instruments which produce sound by means of the plucking, striking or bowing of a string, which in most cases is than amplified by a sound-box of varying proportions.

**study** (French equiv: étude) An instrumental piece written primarily as a training aid to the student of a particular instrument. Most studies have little intrinsic musical value, although such works by Chopin, Debussy etc stand on their own merits as compositions as well as being fine training pieces.

**subdominant** The fourth note of the major or minor scale above the tonic.

**submediant** The sixth note of the major or minor scale above the tonic.

**suite** The name originally applied to an instrumental composition in several movements, all of which were in the same key. Later, after the development of the sonata and symphonic forms, the suite was re-defined and came to mean loosely-connected collection of instrumental pieces or excerpts.

**supertonic** The second note of the major or minor scale above the tonic.

**swell** A device on the organ used to increase or diminish the volume.

**sympathetic strings** Strings which are unplayed on a stringed instrument, but which vibrate with the resonance set off by the played strings, thus adding to the overall ambience of sound.

**symphonic poem** A term utilized by Romantic composers in particular to describe an orchestral work based on a non-musical inspiration.

**symphony** Since the time of Haydn, the term has come to mean a serious work for orchestra of substantial size and usually cast in the shape of a sonata. Most symphonies have four movements, including a scherzo, adagio and finale.

**syncopation** A displacement of the beat or rhythmic pulse in music so that the accent falls on the weaker beats.

# T

**tablature** Notation used in 16th and 17th centuries in which the pitch was indicated by letters or numbers.

**tacet** A direction indicating that an instrument or section in a piece is silent for a while – for example, during a movement.

**Tafelmusik** Music written specifically to be played at banqueting occasions. Telemann composed the most famous series of pieces for such occasions.

**tambour** French for drum.

**tambourine** A small single-headed drum, usually hand-held and struck by the palm of the hand or by sticks. It has metal discs set in the frame at regular intervals to produce a jingling sound when shaken.

**tango** A dance of Argentinian origin arriving in Europe just prior to World War I, although there is evidence to suggest that it was taken to South America by African slaves centuries before.

**tanz** German for dance.

**tarantella** A fast 18th-century dance in 6/8 time which gathers momentum as it progresses. It comes from Taranto in Southern Italy.

**tedesca** (Italian) German; for example, *alla tedesca* – in the German manner.

**temperament** The 'tempering' of the musical intervals in the natural scale so that they will sound in tune in all keys and combinations of notes. The equal-temperament scale was first introduced in J S Bach's time, and he quickly became its greatest advocate.

**tempo** Time, or speed; usually used in conjunction with other words, for example tempo di menuetto, if used as a direction to players.

**tenor 1** The highest of the three natural ranges for the male voice, the others being baritone and bass. **2** The corresponding instruments in instrumental families, for example, the tenor recorder, tenor saxophone; the usual range is an octave either side of middle C.

**ternary form** A musical form in which there are three basic sections, the third of which is a recapitulation of the first, either exactly or with slight variations. Commonly represented as ABA.

**tessitura** (Italian for texture) The prevailing compass of notes, or range, in a particular voice; thus a singer is said to have high tessitura, or a piece is of high tessitura.

**tetrachord** A scale of four notes, the interval between the first and last note being a fourth.

**theme song** A song or melody in a large work for stage, radio or screen which is used as an identifying motif.

**third** The interval of a third comprises four semitones for a major third, while a minor third is made up of three semitones.

**through-composed** A term applied to songs when they have different music for each verse, rather than the strophic song which repeats earlier material. German: durchkomponiert.

**time** A word used in music to classify the basic rhythmic patterns, based on the number of beats in a bar: hence we have 4/4 time, 2/4 time, 6/8 time and so fourth. The accents within the bar also determine the precise type of time being used.

**time signature** The indication at the beginning of a composition as to the kind of time used in it. This consists of two numbers, written somewhat in the fashion of a fraction, the lower figure indicating the kind of notes the bar is divided into, while the upper figure shows the number of notes of that type within the bar.

**timpani** Kettledrums.

**toccata** A single-movement instrumental piece in free style and tempo, and designed to display the player's agility. Later times modified the meaning of the term, and it came to include several-movement pieces as well.

**ton** Used in both German and French, it means note, or sound.

**tone 1** The actual quality or distinctive quality of a musical sound. **2** A note from which all overtones have been eliminated, thus supplying a pure representation of a particular pitch. **3** The interval in a scale consisting of two semitones.

**tone colour** The tonal quality inherent in a particular instrument or voice – the precise registration of which is dictated by the number of overtones which are set up by the production of a pitched sound.

**tone poem** The term is the equivalent of the symphonic poem.

**tonic** This is the first note in a given scale: it is also called the keynote.

**tonic sol-fa** This is the musical notation applicable to the solmization system. The tonic sol-fa was invented by John Curwen in the 1840s.

**transcribe** To make an arrangement of a musical work for a performing group or instrument other than the original.

**transpose** To notate or perform music at a pitch other than the original.

**transposing instrument** A musical instrument which is pitched in a key other than C major; that is, to play C major scale in concert pitch on the transcribing instrument would be in reality to play another scale. For example, the tenor saxophone is pitched in B-flat, and so to play the concert C major scale, the player would have to play the instrument's D scale.

**treble 1** A high voice, usually used to describe a prepubescent boy's voice, the equivalent adult voice being a soprano. **2** The highest part in a composition, or the highest part in a choir of mixed voices. **3** High-pitched members of the instrument families.

**tremolo** A rapid reiteration of a note, or a rapid alternation between two notes, thus being primarily a fluctuation of intensity, not of pitch.

**trill** Two notes adjacent to each other which are rapidly alternated.

**trio 1** A work for three voices or instruments. **2** A group made up of three voices or instruments. **3** The middle section of a 17th-century march or minuet was referred to as a trio, being scored for three parts.

**triple concerto** A concerto intended for three solo instruments and orchestra.

**triple time** A musical time in which the primary division is into three beats; for example, 3/4 or 3/2.

**triplet** A group of three notes, of equal time value, played or executed in the space of two notes.

**tritone** The interval of three tones.

**trombone** A long, tubed brass instrument normally without valves. A slide increases or decreases the length of tubing, thus affording the player the full chromatic range of pitches. The valve trombone has a fixed slide and three valves, however, to achieve the complete harmonic range over two octaves. There is a full family covering the usual range of pitches.

**troppo** Too much. This term usually appears in musical scores in the qualifying phrase, *non troppo;* for example, *allegro non troppo* – fast, but not too fast.

**trumpet** A brass instrument with a cylindrical bore which has three transverse valves to regulate and alter the length of tubing so as to produce a full range of tones. The player uses the lips and tongue on the mouthpiece for vibration and articulation.

**(alla) turca** In the Turkish style. This was a term used in the 18th century when the influence of Turkish music was particularly strong in Western Europe.

**tutti** All. A direction in a score to indicate that all the players are required to play.

# U

**unison** A united sounding of the same passage, or note, by more than one instrument or voice, thus singing in unison. In 'octave' unison, the united soundings are an octave apart.

**up-beat** The beat represented by the upward movement of the conductor's stick or hand; that is, the beat preceding the main accent. The up-beat is also termed the 'weak' beat.

**up bow** The bowing of a stringed instrument where the action starts at the bow's point and proceeds to the heel of the bow.

**utility music** The notion of utility music, propounded by a group of German composers in the 1920s, that there should be a simple, disciplined style of composition written specifically for the amateur to play at home. It avoids excessive technical demands and any special emphasis on a single performer in the group.

# V

**valsé** French for waltz.

**valve** A mechanism on a brass instrument, used to change the length of tube available. When raised or depressed, it alters the set of overtones (the so-called 'harmonic series'). A combination of three valves gives a brass player the complete chromatic scale over a number of octaves.

**vamping** An improvised accompaniment which consists of a series of simple chords. An instruction book on this type of accompaniment is called a 'vamping tutor'.

**variation(s)** Variations consist of successive remodellings and restatements of the original theme, with the changes taking place in melody, harmony and rhythm. The concept of variation on a theme is a cornerstone of musical composition.

**vaudeville** Originally a type of satirical French song from the Normandy area. Later, it was sung at the end of a spoken drama: Mozart incorporated a vaudeville into his opera *The Seraglio*. By the middle and late 19th century, however, the meaning had broadened to signify a series of songs and dances. By the 20th century vaudeville was simply another word for music hall.

**veloce** Quickly. A direction requiring uninterruptedly smooth and swift execution of a musical piece or passage, rather than any speed increase.

**verbunkos** A Hungarian dance used by soldiers to entice recruits into the army. Most popular in the early 19th century, it later inspired such composers as Liszt, Bartók and Kodaly.

**verismo** Realism. The term is used to describe the Italian opera introduced by such composers as Mascagni, Puccini and Leoncavallo at the turn of the 20th century. In contrast to earlier operas, which revolved round romantic, mythological or fantastic characters and situations, *opera verismo* had plots firmly based in realistic, often squalid, contemporary settings, with down-to-earth characters.

**vibrato** A rapid and even fluctuation in the pitch of a note either sung or played. When exaggerated by a singer, it is termed a 'wobble'.

**vielle 1** A medieval fiddle. **2** French for hurdy-gurdy.

**vihuela** A plucked string instrument with a fingerboard, originally from Spain. The body was guitar-shaped, and strings arranged as on a lute. Popular during the Renaissance, it gave way to the guitar in about 1700.

**villancico** A Spanish song of the 16th century, containing a number of verses with refrains between each one.

**villanella** A rustic part-song with its origins in 16th century Italy.

**villanelle** French setting of a poem – similar to the Italian villanella, though with significant differences in detail.

**viol** Forebear of the violin family, superseded by them in the 18th century. They are similar in shape to the violin, though with shoulders coming away from the instrument's neck at a more acute angle. The fingerboard has frets, and a different bowing technique is required. The viol has enjoyed a recent return to popularity with the rise in interest in performance of older music on original instruments.

**violin family** This is a family of four-stringed, unfretted, bowed instruments. They are generally thought to have evolved in the 16th century out of the fiddle and its related ancestors. In Europe, by the middle of the 18th century, the family was supreme among stringed, bowed instruments, and still is today. The present-day family includes the violin, the highest-pitched of the group; the viola, some 3in (10cm) longer than the violin; the violoncello (or 'cello), played sitting down rather than from the shoulder; and the double bass.

**virginal(s)** A keyboard instrument and a member of the harpsichord family, smaller than a harpsichord and oblong in shape, with the keyboard runnning along the longer side of the case.

**virtuoso** A performer with complete technical mastery of an instrument.

**vivo** Lively, or fast.

**vocalise** A wordless vocal composition chiefly employing vowel sounds. Vocalises have been written for both concert performances and practice purposes.

**voce** Voice. Many musical directions include this word; for example *colla voca* – with the voice; *sotto voce* – subdued in tone (literally, 'under the voice').

**voice 1** Sounds produced by the human vocal chords. **2** A part, or strand, in harmony or counterpoint, whether sung or played.

**volante** Fast and light.

**volkslied** A popular (or folk) song.

**volti** Turn – an instruction to turn the page when reading sheet music.

**voluntary** Most commonly, an organ piece played before or after a church service, either written or improvised. Voluntaries for other instruments always involve an element of improvisation.

**vorspiel** Literally, 'before-play'; a prelude or an overture, especially in opera.

**vuota** Empty – for example, *scorda vuota* – an instruction to play an open string.

# W

**waits 1** In the Middle Ages, townspeople employed to sound the hours and give other signals. Later, organized groups of musicians who sang and played tunes in or around a town. **2** An old instrument, from the shawm family, played by the waits.

**waltz** A triple-time dance, originating in Austria and Germany in the 18th century, based on a folk dance called the Ländler.

**Weihnachtsoratorium** A Christmas oratorio.

**whole-note** In the USA, a *semibreve*.

**whole-tone scale** A scale in which all the intervals, or steps, between the notes are whole tones, as opposed to the diatonic scale which combines whole-tone and half-tone steps, and the chromatic, which is exclusively half-tone steps. The whole-tone scale thus has six different notes, although only two such scales are possible (one starting on C, the other on D-flat). Each scale can be begun at any point, as there is no keynote. This scale has been used by many 20th century composers.

**wind band** A band made up of mixed wind instruments, usually accompanied by percussion. It differs from brass bands in that woodwinds are included as well.

# X

**xylophone** A tuned percussion instrument made up of two rows of wooden bars arranged in the same manner as a piano keyboard. The bars are struck with beaters.

# Z

**zarzuela** A traditional Spanish comic opera, usually with spoken dialogue in part, and with a strong element of folk song.

**zither** A stringed instrument native to Central Europe, with some strings vibrating at a fixed pitch, and others stopped with a finger to produce the melody. It is played across the lap.

# Bibliography

G. Abraham, *The Concise Oxford History of Music,* Oxford University Press, Oxford, 1979

G. Abraham (ed), *New Oxford History of Music* (10 vols), Oxford University Press, Oxford, 1957–74

G. Abraham, *Studies in Russian Music,* Ayer & Co, Salem, 1935

W. Apel, *The Harvard Brief Dictionary of Music,* Harvard University Press, Cambridge, 1969

D. Arnold, *Giovanni Gabrieli and the Music of the Venetian High Renaissance,* Oxford University Press, Oxford, 1979

D. Arnold et al, *The New Grove Italian Baroque Masters,* Norton, New York, 1984

D. Arnold (ed), *The New Oxford Companion to Music,* Oxford University Press, Oxford, 1983

W. Austin, *Music in the 20th Century,* Norton, New York, 1966

A. Bachmann, *An Encyclopedia of the Violin,* Da Capo, New York, 1975

H. Barlow and S. Morgenstern, *A Dictionary of Musical Themes,* Crown, New York, 1948

E. Borroff, *Music of the Baroque,* Da Capo, New York, 1978

P. Boulez, *Boulez on Music Today,* Faber and Faber, London, 1979

N. Butterworth, *Music of Aaron Copland,* Universe, New York, 1986

J. Caldwell, *Medieval Music,* Indiana University Press, Bloomington, 1978

A. Chujoy, *The New York City Ballet,* Da Capo, New York, 1981

C. Claghorn, *Biographical Dictionary of American Music,* Nyack, 1974

A. Copland, *Copland on Music,* Da Capo, New York, 1976

J. Davidson, *A Dictionary of Protestant Church Music,* Scarecrow, Metuchen, 1975

A. Einstein, *Essays on Music,* Norton, New York, 1962

A. Einstein, *Greatness in Music,* Da Capo, New York, 1976

A. Einstein, *A Short History of Music,* Random House, New York, 1954

D. Ewen, *American Composers – A Biographical Dictionary,* Putnam Publishing Group, New York, 1982

P. Gammond, *An Illustrated Guide to the Composers of Classical Music,* Arco, New York, 1981

H. Hitchcock and S. Sadie (eds), *The New Grove Dictionary of Music in the United States,* Norton, New York, 1986

A. Hutchings, *The Baroque Concerto,* Faber and Faber, London, 1961

F. Jones, *A Handbook of American Music and Musicians,* Da Capo, New York, 1971

H. Kallman, *Encyclopedia of Music in Canada,* University of Toronto Press, Toronto, 1981

H. Krehbiel, *Music and Manners in the Classical Period,* Longwood Publishing Group, Dover, 1976

P. Lang, *Music in Western Civilization,* Norton, New York, 1940

V. Picerno (ed), *Dictionary of Musical Terms,* Haskell House, New York, 1981

P. Randel, *Harvard Concise Dictionary of Music,* Harvard University Press, Cambridge, 1978

G. Reese, *Music in the Middle Ages,* Norton, New York, 1940

N. Robeck, *Music of the Italian Renaissance,* Da Capo, New York, 1969

J. and E. Roche, *Dictionary of Early Music,* Oxford University Press, Oxford, 1981

H. Rosenthal and J. Warrack, *Concise Oxford Dictionary of Opera,* Oxford University Press, Oxford, 1979

S. Sadie, *Dictionary of Music and Musicians* (2 vols), Macmillan, London, 1981

H. Schonberg, *Lives of the Great Composers,* Norton, New York, 1981

D. Scott, *International Who's Who in Music and Musicians' Directory,* Gale, Detroit, 1985

R. Simpson (ed), *The Symphony* (2 vols), Penguin, Harmondsworth, 1966–7

N. Sloninsky, *Music of Latin America,* Da Capo, New York, 1972

E. Southern, *Music of Black Americans,* Norton, New York, 1983

T. Surette, *Music and Life,* Schirmer, New York, 1965

J. Westrup, *Dictionary of Music,* Dent, London, 1971

J. Westrup and F. Harrison, *Collins Encyclopedia of Music,* Collins, London, 1976

J. Whitlock, *Music Handbook,* Irvington, New York, 1972

# *Index*